CORRELATIONS®
Division

EASY

WILLIAM ROGERS

iUniverse, Inc.
Bloomington

Division - Easy

iUniverse books may be ordered through booksellers or by contacting:

iUniverse
1663 Liberty Drive
Bloomington, IN 47403
www.iuniverse.com
1-800-Authors (1-800-288-4677)

ISBN: 978-1-4759-8357-9 (sc)
ISBN: 978-1-4759-8358-6 (ebk)

Printed in the United States of America

iUniverse rev. date: 03/21/2013

CORRELATIONS

Dear Consumer,

     Congratulations! You have just purchased a one of a kind puzzle that is geared towards education while also having fun. I have worked diligently to create a style of puzzle that is different from the rest and that would stand out easily above all the others. <u>Correlations</u> is a puzzle that is educational and equipped to enhance the minds of others. This style of puzzle originated out of the thought of making math fun. I wanted to create a puzzle that would help people learn or re-learn the basic math concepts and create different levels in which people could try to conquer. <u>Correlations</u> is suitable for all ages of people whether young or old. This puzzle can be formatted for those who want to take it easy and for those who like a little challenge.

     <u>Correlations</u> is like an enhanced mathematical word search. I have enjoyed bringing this new style of puzzle to the market, and I hope you enjoy doing this puzzle as much as I have enjoyed creating it. Nothing is too hard to do if you just set your mind to it. <u>Correlations</u> is going to challenge you when it comes to math and searching for the words within the puzzle. Congratulations once again, and I hope you have a blast on your <u>Correlations</u> journey!

William S. Rogers III

How to Solve Correlations

- The puzzles consist of a 7x7 grid
- Solve the math within the box and try to figure out what letters go where
- You do this by knowing where each letter falls in the alphabet (EX: A=1, K=11, P=16, T=20)
- EX: To find the letter G you would look for 35/5. This comes out to equal 7=G
- Once you figure this out you have to find the words within the puzzle
- EX: GREEK – the words are not all straight or diagonal. As long as the G is touching the R box, the R is touching the E box, the E is touching the E box, and the E is touching the K box then the word is found within the puzzle
- The letters within the puzzles are only used once (**NO ONE LETTER OR BOX CAN BE USED TWICE**)
- All the boxes within the puzzle are not to be filled
- (1) (2) (3) (4) – These are used to identify the words on the Answer Sheets

Take this 7 X 7-square example on this page

35/7=E (4)	49/7=G (4)	54/6	76/4	5/5	36/6	15/5=C (2)
60/12	21/21=A (4)	42/3=N (4)	32/2=P (2)	54/6	45/3=O (2)	100/25
90/5=R (4)	81/9=I (4)	64/8	57/3=S (2)	54/3=R (2)	81/9	18/1
36/2=R (4)	64/8=H (1)	144/12	20/1=T (3)	25/5=E (2)	30/2	100/5
21/3	38/2	60/3=T (1)	18/1=R (3)	60/12=E (1)	60/3	75/5
54/6	54/3=R (1)	60/12	12/6=B (1)	24/24=A (3)	36/2=R (1)	70/10
26/13	24/6	54/6=I (1)	90/9	20/4	30/6=E (3)	72/9=H (3)

WORDS

1. REBIRTH (18, 5, 2, 9, 18, 20, 8)
2. CORPSE (3, 15, 18, 16, 19, 5)
3. HEART (8, 5, 1, 18, 20)
4. EARRING (5, 1, 18, 18, 9, 14, 7)

To start, look for a word that have letters that are not in the other words. The word CORPSE; locate the C first by finding 2 numbers that will turn out to equal 3. There is only one box in this whole puzzle that has multiples that equal 3; in the upper right hand corner. Next, the O box is located with 45/3=O. After this there are 2 boxes which contain multiples that equal R; 54/3 and 18/1. When a situation like this arises in a puzzle, the best thing to do is to plan ahead and look for the other letters in order to figure out which way you should go. From the 18/1 box there is no P connected to this box. The 54/3 box is the only box that has a P connected to it; 32/2=P. Once the P is found within the puzzle there is another situation in which we have to plan ahead in order to find which box is correct. There is 2 boxes that contain the letter S. The box up above with 76/4 and the box below with 57/3. The box located beneath the P box is the only box that had the letter E connected to it with 25/5. Therefore, the letter S beneath the P box is the box that we go with and the letter E is diagonal from this box. The word CORPSE is now found within the puzzle. All the letters have to connect in order for the word to be found within the puzzle. In cases like trying to find the word CORPSE, plan ahead and locate the other letters within the word you are trying to find. After the word CORPSE is found use the Elimination Process (finding a word and not being able to reuse those same boxes over again) if another problem arises like this one.

If one discovers that a word is too hard to find, locate part of the word within the puzzle first, stop, and search for a new word. This often helps because searching for a new word can eliminate some of the boxes that you may have thought were going to be used for the first word you were searching for. There is no guess work that needs to be done when it comes to these puzzles. All you have to do is solve the math, plan ahead, look at the surrounding boxes, and figure out where the words are within the puzzle. Use these tips in order to continue finding the rest of the words within the puzzle.

Additional Tips

- Try to solve the math within the box to find the words within the puzzle
- Try and look for letters that are not in other words
- In puzzles that have similar letters within words, try and find the letters that are the same (It sometimes help to look for a word backwards, starting with the last letter in the word)
- Remember, you can only use a box once; so try and plan ahead

EASY

400/20	15/3	24/6	80/5	76/4	10/2	27/9
30/10	36/2	14/2	35/7	44/11	22/1	50/2
100/4	14/14	36/6	16/4	45/9	100/5	42/2
28/2	12/4	72/8	16/4	14/1	144/12	25/5
45/9	76/4	28/2	50/10	72/8	27/9	64/8
121/11	39/3	48/2	38/2	45/9	144/12	169/13
484/22	36/4	54/6	60/3	361/19	36/2	324/18

WORDS

1. SNIDE
2. ULCER
3. TRANSMIT
4. VIXEN

EASY

14/7	441/21	45/9	100/10	55/5	529/23	400/20
28/2	144/12	169/13	196/14	36/2	225/15	32/2
48/2	33/11	38/2	25/5	63/7	15/3	10/2
18/2	441/21	400/20	36/2	60/5	121/11	169/13
196/14	54/6	100/5	361/19	35/7	90/18	25/5
15/3	24/8	44/44	27/9	46/2	225/15	40/2
12/4	529/23	55/5	56/8	64/8	81/9	121/11

WORDS

1. SLINK
2. TOWER
3. UNCUT
4. WAITER

EASY

121/11	25/5	26/13	49/7	81/9	72/9	9/3
24/4	35/7	45/5	121/11	46/2	361/19	57/3
324/18	38/2	225/15	30/2	64/8	225/15	100/10
144/12	625/25	169/13	21/7	72/6	12/4	39/3
14/7	22/11	60/3	441/21	18/2	144/12	36/2
44/4	50/25	676/26	25/5	45/3	225/15	14/14
225/15	42/2	28/2	27/3	42/7	400/20	529/23

WORDS

1. SOCIETY
2. TOUCH
3. UNIFORM
4. WALLOW

EASY

14/7	20/1	32/4	64/8	100/10	10/5	12/2
12/4	15/5	60/4	144/12	72/8	24/2	21/1
361/19	75/3	84/7	400/20	676/26	28/2	225/15
625/25	25/5	36/2	34/34	18/9	324/18	76/4
12/4	15/5	324/18	54/3	324/18	15/1	144/12
529/23	169/13	11/11	30/6	45/9	144/12	100/10
14/14	14/14	80/4	40/2	48/4	77/7	15/3

WORDS

1. TOLERATE
2. UNROLL
3. SOLITARY
4. WATER

EASY

144/12	15/3	46/2	44/44	26/2	39/13	225/15
625/25	54/6	20/5	25/5	144/12	52/2	81/9
169/13	60/3	196/14	13/13	361/19	36/2	100/10
10/5	13/13	36/3	42/2	56/7	35/7	60/3
11/1	72/8	256/16	400/20	64/8	60/5	72/9
81/9	121/11	76/3	45/3	15/15	56/8	1/1
44/44	45/5	361/19	12/4	441/21	54/6	81/9

WORDS

1. UPSCALE
2. WEALTH
3. TIDAL
4. SOUGHT

EASY

18/2	144/12	256/16	30/5	72/8	63/7	81/9
169/13	225/15	144/12	361/19	34/2	38/2	121/11
14/2	49/7	15/15	72/9	48/3	40/8	9/3
12/12	36/9	72/9	324/18	13/13	529/23	36/2
66/6	400/20	196/14	28/2	45/9	66/66	11/11
12/4	42/14	34/34	6/3	54/6	36/6	32/4
8/2	44/2	529/23	35/7	72/6	57/3	144/12

WORDS

1. SPANISH
2. THREW
3. VANDAL
4. WELFARE

EASY

15/3	225/15	256/16	361/19	42/2	6/2	48/3
100/10	81/9	54/6	225/15	45/5	63/7	46/2
144/12	66/6	10/2	42/7	54/6	48/6	121/11
55/55	30/10	72/8	676/26	36/2	25/5	676/26
625/25	27/3	25/5	12/4	20/4	44/44	12/4
18/6	15/3	40/5	225/15	35/7	32/2	484/22
36/2	76/4	40/2	99/9	361/19	100/10	1/1

WORDS

1. WHEEZE
2. VARIOUS
3. THICK
4. SPECIFIC

EASY

14/2	25/5	625/25	14/14	30/6	676/26	64/8
81/9	48/2	400/20	27/9	60/5	121/11	4/4
46/46	40/2	40/8	4/4	32/2	32/2	30/15
45/3	35/7	80/4	361/19	36/2	45/9	60/4
36/2	324/18	60/5	324/18	144/12	169/13	60/3
256/16	20/4	225/15	15/3	25/5	60/3	72/8
10/2	18/9	484/22	42/7	529/23	64/8	56/8

WORDS

1. SPLATTER
2. TERRACE
3. VERTEX
4. WHITE

EASY

144/12	225/15	20/1	15/3	24/6	72/8	676/26
100/10	44/44	121/11	45/45	64/8	25/5	42/3
28/2	10/5	45/3	25/5	24/8	15/15	32/2
48/3	14/14	57/3	15/5	38/2	324/18	144/12
14/7	15/3	361/19	54/6	15/3	75/3	30/2
225/15	196/14	225/15	324/18	400/20	60/3	121/11
36/2	121/11	26/2	45/3	225/15	676/26	75/3

WORDS

1. SECRET
2. NOISY
3. TABASCO
4. ZEALOT

EASY

45/3	66/6	11/1	21/7	64/8	144/12	72/8
121/11	400/20	225/15	529/23	45/9	80/4	36/2
54/3	72/8	12/12	42/2	36/2	45/3	54/6
60/4	76/4	39/3	34/2	30/6	400/20	80/5
75/5	256/16	35/7	196/14	15/3	25/5	10/5
25/5	20/4	64/8	24/8	35/5	42/7	48/3
225/15	169/13	324/18	484/22	46/2	50/2	256/16

WORDS

1. WRENCH
2. SEQUEL
3. TAMPER
4. PETIT

EASY

35/5	38/2	121/11	54/54	64/8	25/5	72/8
121/11	45/5	21/3	24/6	35/7	45/9	54/6
64/8	45/3	75/5	32/2	27/9	16/8	72/6
48/3	100/10	52/2	441/21	39/3	121/11	9/3
28/4	24/8	36/9	225/15	30/10	34/34	256/16
12/12	169/13	20/4	60/5	12/6	11/11	144/12
256/16	225/15	441/21	361/19	15/3	81/9	400/20

WORDS

1. SEDUCE
2. PABLUM
3. TACKLE
4. ZOMBIE

EASY

121/11	39/2	289/17	225/15	52/2	64/8	72/8
196/14	400/20	26/2	42/3	121/11	11/11	56/7
63/9	529/23	25/25	256/16	100/10	10/5	16/4
4/2	225/15	9/3	441/21	45/5	324/18	225/15
256/16	16/4	28/2	196/14	48/3	42/3	40/8
50/10	361/19	32/4	24/8	324/18	35/7	60/3
529/23	36/2	20/4	26/2	45/9	361/19	46/2

WORDS

1. PINCH
2. TAUPE
3. SEMESTER
4. WONDER

EASY

100/10	81/9	121/11	45/5	63/7	169/13	14/7
66/6	12/12	42/14	32/8	225/15	35/7	6/2
12/3	15/5	14/14	20/5	72/6	529/23	38/2
256/16	144/12	27/3	20/4	18/9	256/16	225/15
324/18	46/2	33/33	14/14	324/18	38/2	54/3
18/9	99/9	72/8	14/7	54/54	400/20	76/4
42/7	36/6	484/22	54/6	36/2	12/4	15/5

WORDS

1. SPREAD
2. VIABLE
3. TRIBAL
4. WIDOW

EASY

676/26	38/2	625/25	49/7	15/3	16/8	10/2
100/10	121/11	289/17	256/16	14/7	225/15	36/2
57/3	64/8	42/2	54/6	55/5	36/3	81/9
34/17	289/17	361/19	44/44	28/2	40/8	676/26
26/2	33/3	81/9	441/21	36/2	54/54	529/23
121/11	484/22	324/18	20/4	169/13	72/8	10/2
6/3	12/4	60/3	144/12	196/14	24/8	25/5

WORDS

1. SQUARE
2. VISIBLE
3. TRUNK
4. WINCE

EASY

100/10	81/9	72/9	9/3	15/3	25/5	36/6
36/4	44/4	40/8	144/12	28/2	15/3	324/18
12/12	14/7	289/17	324/18	16/4	48/6	25/5
529/23	44/2	225/15	28/2	32/8	24/6	60/3
48/3	225/15	21/7	42/2	42/3	15/5	72/8
144/12	76/4	121/11	81/9	169/13	39/3	36/2
40/5	63/7	400/20	81/9	100/10	12/12	529/23

WORDS

1. MUDDLE
2. SCORN
3. TINDER
4. WRITHE

EASY

72/8	72/6	33/33	64/8	121/11	225/15	42/3
256/16	15/5	36/2	88/8	144/12	54/54	64/8
14/2	17/17	81/9	15/3	256/16	48/4	10/2
100/10	625/25	676/26	80/4	441/21	48/6	81/9
49/7	4/2	45/3	27/9	361/19	75/3	25/5
60/5	100/5	32/8	76/4	63/9	84/7	169/13
21/21	20/4	60/4	49/7	21/3	24/4	25/5

WORDS

1. SCULL
2. MYSTICAL
3. TOGGLE
4. YODEL

EASY

256/16	75/3	15/3	144/12	169/13	48/3	400/20
60/3	60/5	20/4	400/20	33/33	529/23	56/8
484/22	46/2	22/11	60/3	100/4	196/14	121/11
45/9	63/7	15/15	12/12	18/9	14/2	54/6
41/41	225/15	256/16	169/13	324/18	75/3	42/7
36/6	441/21	44/2	12/3	44/44	42/2	529/23
44/2	45/3	45/5	361/19	576/24	24/6	12/12

WORDS

1. PAYABLE
2. SAYING
3. OVOID
4. MATTE

EASY

81/9	42/3	225/15	28/2	100/10	15/3	16/2
54/54	26/2	16/4	42/21	54/9	64/8	121/11
256/16	60/4	38/2	45/9	57/3	225/15	52/2
42/3	39/3	15/3	44/44	169/13	45/3	256/16
60/5	324/18	35/7	54/6	144/12	56/7	60/4
75/3	484/22	196/14	45/3	169/13	225/15	48/3
81/9	9/3	35/7	40/2	12/4	15/1	324/18

WORDS

1. SAINT
2. PHLOEM
3. OBSERVE
4. MODEM

EASY

55/55	66/6	12/4	25/5	42/6	81/9	121/11
49/7	225/15	28/2	361/19	256/16	34/17	12/2
28/2	25/5	28/2	72/8	625/25	18/9	100/10
144/12	45/3	15/15	144/12	400/20	45/9	169/13
256/16	32/2	324/18	42/3	80/4	529/23	44/2
48/2	14/14	30/6	72/6	225/15	42/3	45/3
72/6	57/3	84/7	91/91	121/11	169/13	8/4

WORDS

1. PANSY
2. ONLINE
3. METTLE
4. SARONG

EASY

20/2	256/16	144/12	45/3	60/12	144/12	225/15
100/10	18/3	36/2	15/5	44/2	225/15	45/9
529/23	15/3	121/11	15/3	64/8	484/22	36/2
81/9	33/33	77/7	361/19	20/4	45/45	63/9
14/2	27/9	44/44	30/2	324/18	28/2	400/20
35/5	42/6	64/8	12/3	16/4	76/4	60/4
63/7	72/8	88/8	45/3	54/6	43/43	169/13

WORDS

1. SADIST
2. OVERDO
3. MONGREL
4. PREACH

EASY

12/3	15/5	25/5	84/7	25/5	121/11	225/15
256/16	42/6	57/3	11/11	88/8	625/25	256/16
52/2	48/3	48/4	324/18	441/21	35/7	35/7
64/8	42/3	14/14	28/2	76/4	33/11	20/4
12/12	256/16	39/3	45/3	36/4	42/2	72/6
324/18	57/3	361/19	144/12	76/4	48/3	25/5
24/4	169/13	15/15	54/6	39/3	121/11	100/10

WORDS

1. USUAL
2. SIMPLE
3. PARSLEY
4. MALICE

EASY

100/5	25/5	24/6	27/9	9/3	576/24	12/12
225/15	32/2	56/7	38/2	81/9	25/5	256/16
144/12	169/13	14/14	361/19	14/7	44/44	36/2
49/7	48/8	54/9	44/44	18/2	361/19	45/3
18/6	14/7	169/13	15/3	60/3	12/12	48/2
15/15	38/2	225/15	28/2	11/11	39/3	48/3
81/9	36/2	225/15	121/11	256/16	35/5	54/5

WORDS

1. SMASH
2. MANOR
3. PASTA
4. XEROX

EASY

28/2	625/25	144/12	15/15	16/8	63/7	45/3
60/4	72/6	11/11	84/12	144/12	16/2	48/3
63/9	100/10	26/2	39/3	196/14	26/2	35/7
225/15	169/13	256/16	76/4	15/15	33/33	361/19
76/4	36/2	20/4	324/18	57/3	27/9	14/14
121/11	42/6	529/23	54/6	361/19	36/6	225/15
36/4	361/19	9/3	32/4	77/7	15/5	10/2

WORDS

1. MARSH
2. YAMMER
3. PEACOCK
4. SWISS

EASY

529/23	48/2	441/21	24/6	72/8	121/11	76/4
15/15	24/6	42/7	42/3	45/3	24/8	60/5
12/12	400/20	22/11	15/3	12/4	15/3	144/12
169/13	225/15	196/14	39/3	32/2	324/18	256/16
45/5	32/8	60/5	400/20	44/44	45/9	40/8
45/3	60/3	14/14	20/1	81/9	256/16	34/17
12/3	324/18	10/5	33/11	15/3	81/9	72/9

WORDS

1. SCEPTIC
2. UNBOLT
3. PERCENT
4. MATADOR

EASY

441/21	256/16	72/8	484/22	42/2	529/23	100/10
16/16	15/3	144/12	36/2	225/15	100/5	169/13
484/22	46/2	25/5	48/3	30/6	48/2	400/20
12/3	32/16	324/18	56/7	361/19	196/14	48/3
60/5	45/3	25/5	55/55	40/2	35/7	60/4
81/9	44/2	15/3	76/4	46/2	81/9	529/23
121/11	80/4	169/13	24/2	12/4	529/23	25/5

WORDS

1. SERPENT
2. WITHER
3. TEASE
4. PIVOT

EASY

56/7	64/8	400/20	40/8	14/2	256/16	45/3
225/15	45/3	48/4	121/11	45/3	289/17	77/7
44/2	54/6	28/2	324/18	42/3	21/7	45/3
36/2	361/19	529/23	169/13	55/55	529/23	100/10
10/2	15/3	28/2	144/12	11/11	39/3	84/7
32/4	11/11	20/4	64/8	32/2	81/9	144/12
60/3	80/4	169/13	28/2	76/4	42/3	56/8

WORDS

1. PLANKTON
2. TENSILE
3. SHAMROCK
4. WEATHER

EASY

36/3	42/7	256/16	48/8	121/11	15/3	24/6
256/16	15/3	144/12	225/15	324/18	38/2	36/2
45/3	60/3	60/12	45/9	32/4	144/12	60/5
169/13	361/19	12/12	72/8	15/3	45/45	42/3
25/5	40/2	48/3	324/18	15/5	44/2	529/23
484/22	21/7	625/25	441/21	81/9	42/7	42/2
121/11	400/20	196/14	36/4	36/6	39/3	100/4

WORDS

1. SHERIFF
2. PLEAT
3. TYPICAL
4. INCEST

EASY

400/20	361/19	169/13	42/3	25/5	625/25	144/12
225/15	75/3	44/44	196/14	24/8	48/3	45/5
63/7	144/12	27/3	48/8	25/5	54/6	529/23
76/4	54/3	16/8	28/2	14/2	144/12	256/16
48/3	361/19	81/9	36/2	45/3	60/5	12/4
64/8	81/9	72/9	441/21	72/8	256/16	18/9
169/13	42/3	400/20	225/15	324/18	15/3	28/2

WORDS

1. INFAMY
2. POLICY
3. TURBINE
4. SHORE

EASY

441/21	40/2	45/3	225/15	36/2	60/3	100/5
100/4	15/3	32/4	14/7	48/6	15/3	256/16
144/12	10/2	76/4	81/9	144/12	169/13	45/3
60/5	676/26	625/25	196/14	36/3	400/20	48/4
90/10	20/4	27/3	529/23	88/8	35/7	54/54
54/3	361/19	48/3	225/15	32/4	361/19	42/3
225/15	100/5	324/18	12/12	256/16	28/2	20/1

WORDS

1. INSHORE
2. SHOWY
3. TRAPEZE
4. POTENT

EASY

625/25	676/26	20/4	46/23	81/9	42/3	225/15
45/9	55/11	144/12	35/5	40/8	60/3	15/3
324/18	56/8	100/5	15/3	169/13	361/19	625/25
54/3	72/8	42/6	60/3	45/9	21/3	63/7
121/11	39/3	42/2	441/21	324/18	400/20	225/15
441/21	100/10	529/23	32/4	36/2	48/3	144/12
484/22	75/3	100/5	400/20	57/3	72/8	12/12

WORDS

1. JUGGLE
2. PRESTIGE
3. TRILOGY
4. SHUTTER

EASY

21/7	15/3	169/13	100/10	38/2	144/12	225/15
256/16	225/15	45/3	60/5	72/8	26/2	36/3
20/1	121/11	21/7	400/20	15/15	81/9	676/26
75/3	27/9	100/4	56/8	63/7	100/5	12/4
21/3	15/3	196/14	76/4	324/18	64/8	42/2
44/2	54/6	48/3	121/11	45/3	225/15	80/4
529/23	48/2	35/5	32/4	60/3	36/2	256/16

WORDS

1. SITCOM
2. KNIGHT
3. TROUT
4. PROSPECT

EASY

57/3	60/3	44/2	32/2	529/23	14/2	60/4
81/9	20/1	9/3	11/11	169/13	100/10	49/7
42/7	14/14	441/21	256/16	14/14	54/6	361/19
45/3	144/12	36/2	39/3	60/5	42/6	44/4
60/3	63/7	81/9	77/7	196/14	20/4	54/54
324/18	57/3	48/3	121/11	44/44	529/23	54/3
12/3	3/1	43/43	324/18	15/3	60/3	25/5

WORDS

1. MAGNATE
2. TULIP
3. PAPRIKA
4. SKEWER

EASY

400/20	361/19	46/2	45/3	144/12	60/5	169/13
169/14	48/3	57/3	225/15	34/2	15/3	54/3
256/16	45/9	9/3	76/4	169/13	484/22	529/23
75/3	144/12	225/15	25/5	100/5	441/21	100/4
45/5	36/3	44/4	28/2	80/4	36/2	72/9
48/4	12/12	36/4	15/5	324/18	361/19	45/3
9/3	88/8	36/6	35/7	27/3	256/16	64/8

WORDS

1. CONIFER
2. LEMUR
3. HOSTESS
4. PICKLE

EASY

27/3	15/3	256/16	28/2	100/10	24/6	32/8
56/8	441/21	484/22	72/6	44/44	56/8	529/23
48/2	324/18	76/4	40/2	45/5	36/9	30/6
42/6	55/55	324/18	60/4	484/22	196/14	45/9
66/6	196/14	225/15	25/5	15/3	42/3	15/5
225/15	42/7	32/4	26/2	42/2	225/15	32/4
49/7	81/9	60/3	45/3	39/3	289/17	121/11

WORDS

1. LIVER
2. FOOTAGE
3. QUOTH
4. COMMEND

EASY

441/21	225/15	45/3	25/5	84/7	18/6	144/12
256/16	34/2	32/16	22/11	81/9	45/3	60/5
169/13	39/3	18/9	169/13	35/7	60/5	56/7
64/8	88/8	14/14	1/1	32/2	44/44	20/4
26/2	324/18	5/1	45/45	324/18	196/14	24/8
21/3	9/3	12/4	63/9	144/12	45/9	48/4
54/3	361/19	100/10	38/2	36/2	11/11	12/4

WORDS

1. RABBLE
2. LAPEL
3. ENLARGE
4. CERAMIC

EASY

28/4	25/5	169/13	46/2	44/2	15/5	625/25
676/26	44/44	324/18	256/16	39/39	32/16	42/3
10/5	21/7	30/6	24/8	40/2	63/9	45/5
144/12	625/25	196/14	12/6	12/4	144/12	256/16
225/15	36/2	100/5	36/4	15/15	441/21	84/7
75/3	10/5	54/9	36/2	25/5	16/8	45/3
225/15	20/4	169/13	32/8	16/2	42/7	18/9

WORDS

1. FIBER
2. PUBERTY
3. CATCALL
4. EMBRYO

EASY

36/9	21/7	169/13	42/3	25/5	40/2	45/9
225/15	75/3	11/11	45/3	66/6	32/4	48/2
41/41	64/8	361/19	32/8	44/44	40/2	18/9
42/2	18/6	15/3	16/4	441/21	324/18	60/3
529/23	44/44	48/2	28/2	15/3	20/4	21/7
20/5	16/8	14/14	81/9	12/12	196/14	72/9
100/10	35/7	121/11	100/4	225/15	39/3	48/3

WORDS

1. ANDAHTE
2. BAYONET
3. CASCADE
4. EXTRUDE

EASY

35/7	72/8	256/16	361/19	54/3	676/26	19/19
75/5	529/23	25/5	39/3	32/2	38/2	60/5
144/12	76/4	256/16	30/2	15/15	256/16	51/51
14/2	21/7	42/2	144/12	9/3	64/8	6/3
26/2	14/2	36/2	14/14	40/8	55/55	12/6
30/2	12/4	36/2	324/18	36/4	11/11	36/2
42/7	225/15	72/8	48/4	144/12	625/25	17/17

WORDS

1. ELAPSE
2. CIRRUS
3. BALLROOM
4. ALPHARAY

EASY

625/25	42/6	42/3	225/15	12/4	63/7	169/13
676/26	40/2	100/4	324/18	169/13	144/12	10/5
100/5	32/4	60/4	54/6	39/3	35/7	81/9
144/12	324/18	15/5	48/3	81/9	9/3	144/12
75/3	28/2	25/5	225/15	36/2	60/5	14/2
24/6	30/6	40/5	30/10	4/2	42/3	15/15
6/2	50/2	54/3	54/6	100/5	15/3	16/8

WORDS

1. ENCIRCLE
2. CRIMP
3. BIMONTHLY
4. ANTIHERO

EASY

144/12	45/3	35/7	42/3	15/5	80/4	48/3
256/16	324/18	625/25	42/3	20/4	20/4	324/18
38/2	15/3	25/5	81/9	72/6	225/15	14/14
144/12	121/11	32/2	63/7	48/8	169/13	196/14
225/15	289/17	18/6	39/3	18/9	54/9	46/2
484/22	576/24	441/21	24/6	45/3	15/5	30/6
25/5	35/75	10/5	14/2	16/16	42/7	48/8

WORDS

1. AMBIENCE
2. BUCKEYE
3. COMPILE
4. EFFORT

EASY

42/3	25/5	45/3	144/12	64/8	18/9	56/8
100/10	42/6	256/16	33/33	34/2	84/7	625/25
35/7	81/9	144/12	33/3	169/13	225/15	36/18
441/21	529/23	441/21	36/2	46/2	36/2	46/2
45/3	72/6	225/15	39/3	11/11	15/15	35/7
84/12	42/3	16/8	72/8	40/2	324/18	20/4
15/3	225/15	25/5	81/9	63/9	196/14	8/4

WORDS

1. RATION
2. GLOWER
3. OAKUM
4. NEARBY

EASY

42/2	529/23	14/14	144/12	46/2	484/22	10/2
144/12	12/4	11/11	196/14	169/13	256/16	42/3
81/9	72/9	30/6	40/2	36/2	144/12	256/16
121/11	39/3	361/19	25/5	42/2	32/4	36/4
169/13	49/7	400/20	75/3	324/18	54/9	324/18
54/3	60/3	45/3	324/18	400/20	20/5	441/21
529/23	225/15	15/5	28/2	15/15	48/2	44/44

WORDS

1. FURNACE
2. CRYSTAL
3. GONAD
4. OTTER

EASY

72/8	9/3	15/3	256/16	35/7	42/7	81/9
144/12	84/7	225/15	21/3	24/8	42/6	9/3
12/4	30/6	625/25	121/11	196/14	42/3	256/16
42/3	28/2	3/1	45/3	48/3	99/9	54/6
43/43	15/5	1/1	42/6	44/2	60/3	63/9
45/3	324/18	32/4	60/5	35/7	72/6	20/4
84/7	63/9	60/12	25/25	14/7	36/9	100/10

WORDS

1. NOVEL
2. LYNCH
3. IGNITE
4. GRACE

EASY

144/12	32/4	225/15	48/3	72/6	25/5	12/12
24/6	40/5	15/5	35/5	35/7	33/33	36/2
27/9	12/12	56/8	80/4	16/4	21/3	100/10
49/7	36/3	676/26	225/15	81/9	52/2	75/5
75/3	196/14	16/16	24/8	324/18	100/5	100/4
12/4	10/10	12/6	4/2	21/7	441/21	256/16
8/2	9/3	40/2	54/6	36/2	289/17	441/21

WORDS

1. CROTCH
2. RADICAL
3. PURITAN
4. GAGGLE

EASY

441/21	256/16	39/3	38/2	36/2	72/8	60/5
256/16	225/15	441/21	45/3	35/7	36/4	76/4
57/3	81/9	17/17	625/25	18/9	16/8	10/5
100/4	121/11	28/2	144/12	36/2	55/55	40/5
39/3	144/12	169/13	44/44	42/7	42/2	256/16
225/15	12/4	36/2	25/5	324/18	361/19	625/25
576/24	42/2	32/16	144/12	40/2	18/9	84/7

WORDS

1. FLYER
2. CRANIUM
3. HUSTLER
4. LIBRA

EASY

60/3	75/3	441/21	44/44	46/2	30/6	44/2
24/2	144/12	36/2	35/7	42/6	169/13	40/8
25/5	35/7	196/14	42/2	30/5	32/4	441/21
169/13	28/2	15/15	225/15	39/3	72/8	42/2
441/21	39/3	45/3	529/23	15/5	44/11	400/20
80/4	72/6	42/2	60/4	225/15	72/6	81/9
144/12	32/4	324/18	256/16	361/19	54/3	20/10

WORDS

1. COURAGE
2. LONELY
3. PODIUM
4. HUMAN

EASY

56/7	42/7	144/12	32/8	225/15	80/4	45/3
60/5	48/8	36/2	21/7	169/13	324/18	25/5
28/2	625/25	225/15	15/15	42/6	45/9	36/2
75/3	52/2	45/45	324/18	63/9	54/6	324/18
12/3	6/3	576/24	48/3	28/2	43/43	81/9
72/8	63/7	45/3	25/5	36/9	64/8	100/10
121/11	55/55	36/2	11/11	72/6	45/9	66/6

WORDS

1. INDEX
2. CORPORAL
3. REGARD
4. GARRET

EASY

45/5	144/12	12/3	81/9	36/2	169/13	80/4
196/14	225/15	66/11	35/7	100/5	36/2	60/5
36/12	24/8	144/12	42/7	45/3	441/21	32/2
121/11	16/8	5/5	18/9	32/16	400/20	42/3
56/7	42/2	81/9	26/2	196/14	324/18	25/5
36/4	34/2	169/13	225/15	15/15	196/14	20/2
60/12	144/12	32/4	12/4	64/8	55/5	45/45

WORDS

1. RAMBLE
2. PUTRID
3. QUAFF
4. CONTORT

EASY

361/19	54/3	144/12	324/18	28/2	45/5	169/13
35/5	45/9	225/15	16/4	42/3	324/18	225/15
289/17	36/2	42/2	12/4	56/8	484/22	46/2
576/24	15/3	15/15	45/3	32/2	225/15	48/3
676/26	60/3	32/2	256/16	144/12	36/6	100/4
90/5	38/2	144/12	81/9	169/13	12/12	15/3
25/5	64/8	196/14	42/7	44/4	54/6	324/18

WORDS

1. GRIND
2. FLOAT
3. NIPPER
4. POPCORN

EASY

42/3	48/3	225/15	16/8	22/11	169/13	36/18
144/12	25/5	361/19	42/6	63/7	36/9	289/17
50/2	48/2	52/2	45/5	28/2	225/15	42/7
32/4	25/5	441/21	20/4	441/21	60/5	42/2
169/13	42/3	76/4	42/6	28/2	11/11	256/16
42/3	144/12	54/6	72/9	35/7	30/2	24/4
15/3	225/15	441/21	196/14	40/2	529/23	676/26

WORDS

1. NEXUS
2. LINEAL
3. MINIS
4. FOUGHT

EASY

57/3	60/3	36/4	72/8	54/3	28/4	100/5
20/5	15/5	484/22	324/18	196/14	30/5	169/13
100/10	45/3	12/2	25/5	225/15	36/6	42//6
144/12	84/7	64/8	529/23	324/18	44/2	529/23
24/4	22/2	42/3	44/2	39/2	56/8	196/14
28/2	38/2	15/15	81/9	20/4	20/4	54/6
121/11	100/10	45/3	72/6	60/5	144/12	196/14

WORDS

1. FORGE
2. LOVING
3. INHERIT
4. JAVELIN

EASY

169/13	45/9	144/12	42/7	256/16	64/8	57/3
256/16	8/2	289/17	25/5	324/18	361/19	42/2
441/21	12/3	42/3	529/23	14/14	66/11	52/2
676/26	72/8	36/4	12/4	36/2	32/4	15/3
15/5	26/2	72/9	36/2	361/19	41/41	72/9
39/3	42/3	100/10	76/4	84/12	11/11	121/11
144/12	169/13	81/9	72/6	60/4	45/15	60/5

WORDS

1. FRENCH
2. GRIDDLE
3. HARASS
4. MISSAL

EASY

54/3	20/4	57/3	40/2	256/16	76/4	121/11
36/2	169/13	27/3	41/41	28/2	64/8	256/16
42/3	56/8	324/18	48/3	225/15	12/2	19/19
34/17	676/26	75/3	324/18	32/8	18/9	10/2
6/2	144/12	30/5	25/5	60/3	441/21	46/2
54/3	42/3	36/2	12/12	196/14	81/9	25/5
30/6	50/5	35/7	529/23	45/9	144/12	64/8

WORDS

1. FRONTIER
2. INTERN
3. JEWEL
4. GRAPH

EASY

80/4	36/2	484/22	441/21	324/18	15/15	42/2
42/3	48/3	225/15	144/12	45/9	169/13	60/5
39/3	256/16	80/4	28/2	361/19	26/2	12/12
100/10	40/2	25/5	27/9	15/15	32/4	49/7
24/6	25/5	56/8	35/7	63/9	20/4	28/2
169/13	43/43	32/8	40/8	11/11	81/9	36/2
225/15	289/17	72/6	13/13	39/3	196/14	60/4

WORDS

1. GENERAL
2. REACTOR
3. LEANING
4. MADAM

EASY

324/18	45/9	42/3	64/8	324/18	38/2	121/11
100/10	35/7	36/2	361/19	25/5	60/3	12/12
65/5	66/11	100/5	45/3	84/7	70/10	144/12
36/4	35/5	441/21	169/13	42/3	225/15	484/22
32/4	28/2	42/2	324/18	529/23	225/15	52/2
676/26	56/56	15/3	75/3	45/9	100/5	56/7
100/4	12/3	144/12	14/7	42/3	32/2	12/12

WORDS

1. GESTURE
2. HONOR
3. REFINE
4. LAUGH

EASY

45/5	361/19	27/9	35/7	361/19	14/7	27/3
21/3	20/4	289/17	24/6	63/7	76/4	22/11
144/12	324/18	169/13	441/21	225/15	441/21	144/12
46/2	484/22	25/5	40/5	60/3	45/9	15/3
18/2	9/3	10/5	42/6	16/8	324/18	256/16
361/19	24/3	225/15	42/7	34/34	54/6	63/9
144/12	42/42	48/6	39/3	225/15	42/3	28/4

WORDS

1. GIRTH
2. HOMAGE
3. QUIBBLE
4. RECESS

EASY

99/11	144/12	45/3	42/3	48/3	18/9	10/2
100/10	121/11	60/5	19/19	15/15	44/2	441/21
529/23	64/8	11/11	27/9	72/6	56/7	45/3
54/3	54/6	45/9	18/1	4/4	39/3	12/6
15/5	24/6	32/8	225/15	25/25	25/5	324/18
45/3	36/2	169/13	42/3	56/8	441/21	60/12
60/5	48/6	40/8	45/5	28/2	12/12	40/5

WORDS

1. MORAL
2. OMEGA
3. PALACE
4. RUNNER

EASY

144/12	56/8	100/10	81/9	45/3	66/6	72/8
18/1	169/13	36/2	196/14	225/15	256/16	44/2
45/3	529/23	8/2	225/15	38/2	25/5	44/4
121/11	46/2	60/3	44/2	144/12	20/5	31/31
60/5	32/8	72/8	441/21	28/2	72/12	36/9
324/18	361/19	8/4	32/16	60/4	289/17	576/24
25/25	15/3	48/6	80/4	18/9	39/3	81/9

WORDS

1. ROTUND
2. PELVIS
3. MOTHER
4. GROWL

EASY

529/23	44/2	12/2	10/10	15/3	144/12	256/16
42/3	100/5	28/4	27/3	21/3	42/2	25/5
25/25	15/3	42/3	169/13	225/15	676/26	324/18
625/25	81/9	76/4	169/13	75/3	196/14	100/4
100/5	361/19	24/6	60/3	45/3	400/20	25/5
441/21	72/6	441/21	28/2	361/19	26/2	36/2
484/22	63/9	12/12	72/9	9/3	54/6	12/2

WORDS

1. MOURN
2. LANDING
3. ISOMER
4. GUSSET

EASY

625/25	64/8	52/2	18/2	324/18	12/3	121/11
169/13	44/4	15/15	36/2	42/3	14/14	225/15
34/2	225/15	60/3	45/3	35/7	324/18	400/20
54/3	34/34	35/7	24/3	43/43	484/22	42/2
529/23	27/3	57/3	66/6	45/3	15/3	121/11
400/20	36/2	144/12	12/6	4/2	25/5	36/2
361/19	18/2	99/11	12/12	45/5	40/5	36/6

WORDS

1. KARAOKE
2. REVERT
3. IRISH
4. HAIRDO

EASY

36/2	42/3	144/12	60/5	48/3	72/12	48/8
169/13	81/9	8/2	196/14	25/5	72/9	39/3
100/10	57/3	35/5	42/3	324/18	15/3	10/5
676/26	27/3	225/15	14/14	361/19	76/4	100/4
100/5	169/13	16/4	60/4	16/2	441/21	9/3
529/23	52/2	20/4	12/2	28/2	11/11	2/1
14/7	64/8	169/13	45/3	144/12	40/5	45/9

WORDS

1. HANDSOME
2. MESCAL
3. PERSON
4. RIGID

EASY

54/3	76/4	12/4	14/2	144/12	60/12	12/6
21/7	27/3	45/9	64/8	15/3	529/23	441/21
44/2	676/26	40/2	676/26	54/6	48/4	46/2
13/13	15/5	17/17	76/4	32/4	42/2	35/7
35/5	27/3	24/3	441/21	28/2	35/7	57/3
30/3	324/18	169/13	18/2	324/18	361/19	30/5
144/12	48/3	225/15	39/3	54/6	42/3	36/4

WORDS

1. HAZEL
2. RUSTIC
3. PROMISE
4. MINUS

EASY

324/18	57/3	100/5	144/12	121/11	32/4	25/5
30/5	42/6	28/2	40/8	25/5	81/9	676/26
75/3	20/4	60/3	24/3	48/4	16/16	36/12
32/8	484/22	45/9	10/2	49/7	169/13	44/2
196/14	144/12	196/14	20/5	20/1	15/3	225/15
45/3	256/16	18/2	60/3	27/3	60/4	18/2
9/3	54/3	25/5	90/10	26/2	56/8	55/5

WORDS

1. HEAVE
2. INVENT
3. MIDGET
4. REPLETE

EASY

144/12	225/15	36/6	42/6	121/11	100/10	28/4
169/13	625/25	54/3	676/26	35/7	14/7	18/2
25/5	32/4	12/12	54/3	18/6	42/3	36/6
34/2	60/3	225/15	28/2	36/9	80/4	10/2
24/8	6/2	20/5	42/3	30/6	15/3	4/4
225/15	42/3	15/3	12/12	48/3	32/4	88/8
441/21	529/23	169/13	196/14	484/22	45/9	75/3

WORDS

1. HENCE
2. NECTAR
3. INTAKE
4. MANOR

EASY

48/3	225/15	48/12	20/5	36/3	169/13	144/12
22/11	32/4	81/9	25/5	35/7	45/9	64/8
72/9	54/3	256/16	54/6	26/2	6/3	225/15
12/4	75/3	169/13	45/3	25/5	20/5	42/2
15/5	40/2	324/18	18/2	42/6	54/3	60/3
20/10	76/4	121/11	15/3	15/3	12/12	196/14
42/3	60/5	72/8	361/19	144/12	225/15	324/18

WORDS

1. IMPEDE
2. RESIST
3. OUTAGE
4. MEMORY

EASY

36/6	121/11	144/12	49/7	25/5	169/13	225/15
75/3	27/3	42/3	144/12	54/3	361/19	45/9
100/5	144/12	12/12	15/3	20/1	12/3	76/4
60/5	75/5	80/4	100/5	57/3	81/9	12/4
225/15	48/3	361/19	36/9	324/18	36/4	15/3
14/7	441/21	49/6	48/3	36/4	35/5	72/6
14/14	169/13	100/10	121/11	64/8	81/9	121/11

WORDS

1. FILTER
2. PRIDE
3. MUSTANG
4. LISTLESS

EASY

76/4	121/11	54/3	60/5	256/16	39/3	54/6
64/8	45/9	57/3	45/5	441/21	54/3	21/3
24/6	18/9	39/3	256/16	81/9	42/3	15/3
84/7	48/3	225/15	361/19	48/3	40/2	12/6
169/13	32/2	196/14	28/4	144/12	45/3	28/2
42/3	60/4	100/5	10/2	60/3	81/9	100/10
100/4	26/2	60/4	9/3	54/3	56/3	12/12

WORDS

1. RIPPLE
2. POSIT
3. OCTOBER
4. IMPULSE

EASY

441/21	46/2	625/25	52/2	625/25	54/3	121/11
169/13	225/15	256/16	32/2	484/22	36/2	60/4
144/12	32/2	42/3	63/7	196/14	20/4	121/11
25/25	25/5	54/3	28/2	13/13	80/4	12/4
100/10	72/8	64/8	56/8	11/11	14/2	27/3
21/7	45/3	324/18	9/3	72/6	16/2	6/3
42/2	42/3	63/7	72/9	48/8	121/11	225/15

WORDS

1. PRIVET
2. ORGAN
3. HICKORY
4. FLANNEL

EASY

32/2	32/4	225/15	256/16	289/17	34/8	8/2
16/8	54/3	144/12	100/5	361/19	60/5	72/12
36/6	75/3	15/3	54/3	72/8	42/7	44/4
20/4	48/8	16/16	36/2	88/11	32/4	100/10
18/1	39/3	324/18	42/3	18/18	25/5	35/7
20/5	48/3	11/11	40/2	15/3	60/3	196/14
144/12	36/2	45/9	42/3	19/19	81/9	121/11

WORDS

1. HISTORY
2. NARRATE
3. PREFER
4. RETAIN

EASY

121/11	44/4	25/5	36/6	32/4	100/10	144/12
169/13	36/2	42/2	625/25	54/3	72/6	76/4
57/3	16/4	12/12	361/19	361/19	441/21	529/23
46/2	225/15	196/14	57/3	42/3	484/22	42/3
42/2	676/26	76/4	15/1	45/3	63/9	75/3
100/4	144/12	10/2	28/2	100/5	15/5	45/9
21/7	49/7	56/7	81/9	12/4	24/3	45/3

WORDS

1. NOTCH
2. LUNGE
3. KUDOS
4. HYSSON

EASY

169/13	45/3	54/3	60/5	72/12	20/4	33/11
144/12	56/8	441/21	35/7	100/4	81/9	256/16
48/3	45/3	36/2	36/18	40/8	40/2	54/6
34/2	36/2	12/6	42/3	25/5	12/4	361/19
441/21	46/2	22/22	28/7	484/22	42/2	9/3
21/7	84/7	36/4	72/9	100/10	54/6	45/3
54/3	76/4	121/11	99/9	18/2	16/8	144/12

WORDS

1. ICEBERG
2. LABOUR
3. JUSTICE
4. KIDNEY

EASY

121/11	9/3	169/13	100/10	256/16	40/8	25/5
21/7	35/5	36/9	45/9	40/8	48/3	42/3
24/4	144/12	12/3	625/25	52/2	324/18	441/21
75/3	54/6	100/5	54/3	80/4	169/13	42/2
90/18	441/21	54/3	24/6	20/4	26/2	42/3
39/3	256/16	75/3	225/15	60/5	25/5	18/2
441/21	529/23	44/2	45/45	484/22	144/12	16/16

WORDS

1. RELAY
2. PRUNE
3. MEDIUM
4. IMMUNE

EASY

39/3	76/4	54/9	42/3	60/5	45/9	100/10
16/2	25/5	441/21	36/3	144/12	81/9	64/8
15/15	57/3	40/2	55/55	27/9	42/2	4/2
24/6	441/21	36/6	45/45	15/3	42/6	54/3
144/12	12/3	18/2	20/4	38/19	60/3	46/2
529/23	15/5	225/15	42/3	361/19	35/7	100/10
10/5	196/14	34/17	28/2	33/11	14/7	27/9

WORDS

1. BACILLUS
2. CONSTRUE
3. AUDIENCE
4. FESTAL

EASY

66/6	225/15	40/8	24/4	121/11	84/7	625/25
39/3	54/3	60/5	60/4	12/6	196/14	64/8
441/21	35/7	529/23	24/6	576/24	39/3	20/4
24/3	361/19	32/4	441/21	324/18	45/9	32/2
42/2	225/15	15/15	35/5	76/4	44/44	45/9
40/8	18/6	15/3	36/2	361/19	21/3	24/8
100/10	10/2	16/2	30/15	4/2	41/41	9/3

WORDS

1. DRAPE
2. COHERE
3. BRASH
4. ASSEMBLY

EASY

76/4	54/3	36/4	32/4	225/15	144/12	169/13
26/2	28/7	16/4	72/8	57/3	42/3	75/3
75/15	40/5	361/19	25/5	36/4	16/16	38/2
33/11	15/5	14/14	55/5	22/11	40/8	256/16
121/11	196/14	48/3	54/3	60/4	45/3	529/23
44/2	225/15	484/22	676/26	54/3	45/3	12/6
52/2	144/12	15/5	15/15	12/3	16/8	63/7

WORDS

1. ABRASION
2. BOOKISH
3. CONCH
4. DROPSY

EASY

52/26	144/12	18/6	256/16	11/11	15/3	361/19
54/3	225/15	289/17	324/18	100/10	14/2	24/6
12/4	48/3	45/3	144/12	18/9	100/4	12/6
24/4	20/10	54/6	21/3	441/21	25/5	42/3
36/9	35/7	45/9	54/3	36/6	12/12	32/16
36/2	256/16	28/2	676/26	625/25	15/3	361/19
63/9	121/11	144/12	25/5	324/18	60/3	39/3

WORDS

1. BURNER
2. COPIER
3. DYNASTY
4. EARLOBE

EASY

324/18	121/11	12/3	121/11	45/9	15/15	12/6
40/8	225/15	46/2	30/6	18/6	72/6	42/3
60/4	144/12	16/16	169/13	225/15	15/5	16/8
12/4	24/6	225/15	25/5	38/2	66/66	32/16
32/4	57/3	48/3	144/12	48/8	75/5	36/2
54/3	361/19	54/6	42/3	12/3	40/2	25/5
28/7	21/3	27/9	441/21	12/12	529/23	11/11

WORDS

1. DEMOLISH
2. CAFTAN
3. BACKWOODS
4. AEROSOL

EASY

32/32	225/15	35/7	20/4	39/3	256/16	24/8
441/21	42/3	60/5	44/2	55/55	225/15	44/4
676/26	12/12	12/4	324/18	24/2	60/5	625/25
169/13	81/9	49/7	225/15	72/6	196/14	289/17
34/2	60/3	484/22	54/3	76/4	441/21	24/12
75/5	15/3	42/2	60/5	48/12	144/12	9/3
6/3	20/5	15/3	27/9	21/3	49/7	64/8

WORDS

1. ANAGRAM
2. BULLOCK
3. CUTICLE
4. DEVOLVE

EASY

49/7	100/10	30/30	36/6	121/11	14/2	12/6
256/16	15/5	42/3	12/4	20/4	16/4	289/17
121/11	25/5	45/3	45/45	40/8	54/3	36/3
72/6	84/12	36/2	25/5	28/2	169/13	42/3
48/3	18/9	60/12	529/23	48/2	80/4	100/5
75/3	100/5	20/5	57/3	34/17	32/4	25/5
8/4	32/8	225/15	42/2	441/21	144/12	21/3

WORDS

1. ACANTHUS
2. BREED
3. DOUBLET
4. CONFER

EASY

60/3	144/12	225/15	36/2	28/2	256/16	54/3
45/3	42/3	72/12	42/2	484/22	20/5	45/9
441/21	75/3	46/2	27/9	20/4	15/5	12/4
529/23	16/16	15/3	484/22	676/26	40/5	196/14
52/2	100/4	324/18	12/2	100/5	25/5	441/21
15/5	12/4	100/10	48/8	35/7	20/5	225/15
15/15	39/3	42/3	54/6	63/9	64/8	22/11

WORDS

1. FECUND
2. DEFRAY
3. CHEVRON
4. BOUNCER

EASY

48/6	441/21	625/25	676/26	80/4	20/4	52/2
169/13	196/14	54/6	15/15	54/3	225/15	24/8
48/3	40/8	39/3	72/6	34/2	42/2	16/16
121/11	12/2	60/4	625/25	12/4	144/12	6/2
196/14	60/3	63/7	72/8	16/8	75/3	64/8
18/9	42/2	144/12	48/3	14/2	49/7	48/2
36/4	45/5	45/45	35/7	35/7	32/4	42/6

WORDS

1. BYLINE
2. CALYX
3. AUTOMAT
4. EPICURE

EASY

48/2	60/5	48/4	169/13	35/5	81/9	49/7
64/8	32/4	225/15	529/23	225/15	24/6	15/3
18/9	324/18	52/2	24/12	16/16	72/6	80/4
42/3	625/25	100/4	54/3	20/10	44/44	26/13
100/5	144/12	625/25	169/13	36/4	529/23	48/2
100/10	36/2	60/4	60/3	24/8	48/48	10/2
77/7	55/11	45/3	18/6	121/11	225/15	16/4

WORDS

1. BLOWZY
2. AIRBORN
3. COMBAT
4. DOCTOR

EASY

9/3	10/2	225/15	100/10	55/55	121/11	80/4
25/5	32/4	36/2	324/18	36/9	361/19	12/12
18/2	15/5	54/3	76/4	81/9	21/3	36/6
49/7	44/44	81/9	15/3	24/6	48/8	42/3
72/9	28/2	14/1	144/12	256/16	289/17	30/6
32/8	529/23	15/5	56/56	676/26	484/22	52/2
484/22	14/2	60/5	144/12	60/4	12/6	18/9

WORDS

1. DISTAFF
2. CLOVEN
3. ERRAND
4. ARSENAL

EASY

54/3	324/18	36/9	76/4	144/12	12/4	42/2
45/9	529/23	18/6	35/7	441/21	100/10	32/4
40/8	15/3	21/7	54/3	28/7	27/3	196/14
144/12	256/16	9/3	361/19	625/25	25/5	60/4
45/3	60/5	42/3	54/6	484/22	72/6	52/2
48/12	36/4	44/2	72/8	12/3	54/54	16/8
14/7	6/3	20/4	49/7	63/7	144/12	30/15

WORDS

1. EVINCE
2. CURSIVE
3. DECREE
4. BLAZON

EASY

45/3	21/7	36/2	361/19	55/55	144/12	225/15
48/3	324/18	20/4	625/25	60/3	35/7	15/3
36/2	10/2	54/3	121/11	45/9	48/3	48/2
30/5	6/3	36/4	144/12	256/16	324/18	45/9
18/9	45/45	54/3	44/44	80/4	15/15	45/5
40/5	44/11	54/54	24/6	48/6	289/17	676/26
75/3	24/12	100/5	100/4	144/12	15/5	196/14

WORDS

1. APPEASE
2. BARBERRY
3. CHALET
4. EXERT

EASY

60/4	32/16	49/7	72/8	100/10	256/16	324/18
361/19	441/21	45/9	12/3	45/45	35/7	42/2
529/23	60/5	55/55	75/3	80/4	169/13	676/26
75/3	56/8	16/2	16/16	42/3	36/2	45/5
55/5	50/10	42/6	196/14	28/2	12/3	16/16
6/3	225/15	56/56	32/2	196/14	45/3	42/7
41/41	2/1	42/3	24/8	48/6	24/6	121/11

WORDS

1. ARMADA
2. CANNY
3. BOGGLE
4. DONATE

EASY

35/7	43/43	36/4	25/5	45/9	21/3	169/13
225/15	48/3	324/18	361/19	32/2	84/7	45/3
60/5	11/11	28/2	48/12	15/3	36/9	48/4
676/26	24/12	42/2	100/5	75/3	36/2	30/6
625/25	54/6	54/54	225/15	15/5	76/4	625/25
10/5	15/3	56/56	196/14	144/12	25/5	289/17
441/21	529/23	44/2	16/4	72/8	46/2	39/3

WORDS

1. COUNSEL
2. EATERY
3. DIESEL
4. ARABIAN

EASY

48/2	441/21	42/6	15/5	144/12	256/16	34/17
289/17	12/3	36/2	76/4	36/3	35/7	54/3
14/2	49/7	54/6	46/2	43/43	42/6	12/12
63/9	64/8	361/19	225/15	144/12	38/2	32/4
45/9	12/6	40/5	44/4	60/3	57/57	57/3
44/44	12/2	441/21	38/2	361/19	12/4	72/8
121/11	6/3	25/5	54/3	676/26	30/6	100/4

WORDS

1. ALGEBRA
2. DISBURSE
3. CLASSIC
4. BESTOW

EASY

25/25	9/3	60/3	15/3	40/8	169/13	25/5
361/19	57/3	72/9	100/10	225/15	30/6	121/11
45/9	256/16	225/15	32/4	484/22	60/5	32/4
21/7	324/18	25/5	43/43	32/8	45/9	81/9
144/12	43/43	196/14	12/6	324/18	20/4	484/22
529/23	48/2	144/12	256/16	15/3	196/14	27/9
28/7	12/3	35/7	36/2	57/3	676/26	100/5

WORDS

1. BEHOLDEN
2. CHORAL
3. DEPRAVE
4. ESTEEM

EASY

39/3	144/12	66/6	54/3	54/54	18/6	225/15
36/2	76/4	42/3	12/4	32/4	24/12	48/3
44/4	225/15	25/5	121/11	81/9	35/7	20/5
81/9	72/6	121/11	76/4	64/8	16/8	54/6
56/7	18/9	10/2	18/6	25/5	100/10	12/12
400/20	441/21	28/2	441/21	36/4	12/3	21/21
46/2	15/5	484/22	529/23	100/10	169/13	42/3

WORDS

1. BECKON
2. CHISEL
3. DEBARK
4. ADJUNCT

EASY

45/5	40/8	60/4	60/3	55/11	49/7	441/21
18/6	12/3	81/9	45/3	54/6	80/4	36/9
441/21	676/26	225/15	529/23	36/9	225/15	42/3
100/4	42/3	529/23	100/5	144/12	24/6	35/7
144/12	15/5	196/14	361/19	21/3	99/11	14/14
36/4	32/16	54/6	10/2	42/2	144/12	16/16
18/9	16/4	10/5	12/6	6/3	49/7	24/8

WORDS

1. ADDITION
2. BENTWOOD
3. CLIENT
4. DISLODGE

EASY

16/4	57/3	24/4	30/6	225/15	45/9	48/3
81/9	28/2	25/5	42/3	12/4	20/4	169/13
361/19	24/6	60/5	54/3	72/12	225/15	66/11
90/18	40/2	15/5	54/54	361/19	21/21	144/12
676/26	75/3	42/7	100/5	35/7	324/18	100/4
121/11	169/13	289/17	529/23	43/43	441/21	48/2
44/2	54/54	44/44	54/6	63/9	15/5	64/8

WORDS

1. FARCE
2. DESIST
3. CARAFE
4. AWESOME

EASY

42/2	15/5	529/23	16/4	64/8	25/5	54/54
72/9	42/3	44/44	14/14	81/9	60/3	361/19
144/12	25/5	32/2	54/3	60/5	12/12	72/12
12/3	15/5	576/24	256/16	44/2	21/7	16/8
41/41	44/4	48/3	144/12	72/8	54/6	63/9
100/10	225/15	121/11	361/19	45/9	196/14	256/16
441/21	52/2	76/4	35/7	169/13	20/4	16/4

WORDS

1. ATAVISM
2. EXPOSE
3. DAPPLE
4. CARIES

EASY

25/5	169/13	48/8	225/15	48/3	81/9	24/6
100/10	121/11	42/6	55/55	36/9	15/5	441/21
35/5	16/8	42/2	55/5	48/6	40/5	42/7
45/9	25/5	54/54	18/2	14/14	54/9	12/3
15/3	24/6	324/18	57/3	15/3	361/19	676/26
60/5	625/25	100/5	32/4	60/3	54/3	80/4
80/4	441/21	36/6	88/8	81/9	20/4	144/12

WORDS

1. BASHFUL
2. CHASTE
3. FAKIR
4. DUFFER

EASY

32/2	196/14	27/3	12/6	45/5	54/3	76/4
49/7	13/13	80/4	64/8	18/2	32/8	144/12
121/11	256/16	15/5	54/3	60/3	72/8	45/3
60/4	72/6	225/15	45/5	42/3	36/3	324/18
361/19	100/10	256/16	196/14	10/2	35/5	35/7
42/3	21/7	121/11	81/9	42/7	30/6	625/25
36/4	9/3	45/3	169/13	60/3	48/3	34/2

WORDS

1. ACONITE
2. DINGY
3. COCKPIT
4. BIRTHING

EASY

121/11	6/3	49/6	36/2	81/9	12/3	100/10
256/16	225/15	35/7	45/3	14/7	24/6	24/2
44/44	28/2	144/12	39/3	32/16	45/45	25/5
28/2	81/9	225/15	441/21	15/5	529/23	484/22
42/3	45/3	441/21	54/3	21/7	42/2	39/3
144/12	25/5	324/18	169/13	225/15	25/5	12/4
60/4	12/6	60/3	196/14	14/14	36/3	45/45

WORDS

1. DACRON
2. CECUM
3. BROILER
4. ANTENNA

EASY

81/9	121/11	625/25	100/5	15/15	100/10	52/2
63/9	72/9	20/4	441/21	24/12	529/23	18/6
44/2	48/4	12/3	30/15	15/5	144/12	21/3
32/8	15/3	36/4	60/4	225/15	81/9	45/9
100/10	100/4	484/22	63/7	40/2	121/11	26/2
196/14	24/2	45/9	24/6	16/4	44/44	289/17
54/3	16/8	76/4	12/2	6/3	4/4	48/2

WORDS

1. DIODE
2. BEVEL
3. CLIMAX
4. ABBOT

EASY

324/18	25/5	63/7	18/6	60/5	144/12	256/16
45/3	625/25	60/5	48/12	40/5	51/51	121/11
289/17	18/9	44/4	44/44	35/7	56/8	22/11
21/3	9/3	361/19	54/3	15/5	25/5	20/5
39/3	42/2	121/11	16/4	144/12	76/4	45/9
100/10	676/26	32/4	529/23	484/22	196/14	35/7
44/2	32/2	21/21	441/21	72/8	40/2	4/2

WORDS

1. LEGAL
2. HUSKY
3. INSET
4. CHARD

EASY

56/7	42/2	529/23	81/9	225/15	21/7	10/10
256/16	30/6	4/2	25/5	45/3	15/3	9/3
289/17	400/20	39/3	60/4	28/2	32/4	20/5
121/11	24/4	20/4	44/2	20/5	225/15	225/15
9/3	49/7	45/3	42/3	54/6	54/3	60/4
48/16	676/26	36/9	15/5	169/13	75/3	324/18
100/4	100/10	20/1	676/26	12/3	35/7	10/5

WORDS

1. EMEND
2. DORMER
3. CONVICT
4. ACHOO

EASY

225/15	25/5	21/7	169/13	100/10	27/9	81/9
63/7	48/4	16/8	144/12	60/4	256/16	676/26
52/2	484/22	529/23	54/3	196/14	75/3	34/34
46/2	72/8	34/34	361/19	34/2	72/6	36/2
36/6	361/19	144/12	441/21	45/3	36/4	50/50
18/9	14/2	76/4	36/6	225/15	81/9	16/4
25/5	16/8	16/4	44/11	56/7	42/7	100/10

WORDS

1. ALOOF
2. BRASS
3. CONSUL
4. DIARY

EASY

169/13	44/4	18/6	42/6	63/7	20/5	12/3
15/3	45/9	45/5	10/2	100/10	121/11	43/43
625/25	196/14	676/26	625/25	80/4	14/14	60/5
441/21	46/2	32/8	54/3	225/15	35/5	144/12
14/7	25/5	21/3	225/15	484/22	15/15	54/54
54/3	54/6	17/17	64/8	196/14	121/11	10/5
45/3	54/3	72/8	20/4	99/9	100/10	12/12

WORDS

1. AORTA
2. CINDER
3. BALLAD
4. ENVOY

EASY

54/3	35/7	36/6	144/12	169/13	100/10	14/7
16/8	35/5	39/3	25/5	27/9	21/7	121/11
256/16	45/3	42/3	56/8	81/9	28/2	144/12
625/25	75/15	100/5	169/13	48/4	36/2	76/4
484/22	15/5	45/3	15/3	54/6	529/23	81/9
100/10	3/1	30/6	16/8	8/4	225/15	16/4
9/3	60/3	72/8	121/11	18/6	56/7	54/9

WORDS

1. BILGE
2. COMIC
3. DOCKET
4. EMOTE

EASY

30/6	13/13	35/5	30/6	4/2	256/16	441/21
625/25	529/23	169/13	100/10	225/15	41/41	15/5
12/3	15/5	30/6	40/5	289/17	43/43	676/26
20/10	72/8	57/3	40/2	441/21	48/3	9/3
64/8	54/6	81/9	32/4	121/11	169/13	35/7
42/3	48/3	196/14	49/7	45/3	60/4	54/3
60/12	144/12	39/3	72/8	12/4	42/6	66/6

WORDS

1. ETHNIC
2. CAPER
3. AMEBA
4. BISHOP

EASY

529/23	54/3	441/21	25/5	27/3	21/7	484/22
81/9	576/24	14/14	52/2	676/26	144/12	625/25
121/11	15/5	44/2	21/3	41/41	24/6	56/8
45/5	5/1	40/8	41/41	16/4	49/7	42/7
36/6	32/16	48/3	42/2	12/4	42/2	15/5
441/21	75/3	15/15	60/5	100/4	12/6	81/9
64/8	30/6	18/6	12/4	14/14	80/4	30/5

WORDS

1. AVARICE
2. BUGGY
3. CAUDAL
4. ECLAT

EASY

40/5	441/21	625/25	676/26	75/3	76/4	225/15
15/3	12/4	12/1	12/4	256/16	6/2	60/5
529/23	484/22	41/41	14/14	35/7	14/14	46/2
42/6	49/7	48/4	54/6	9/3	45/9	56/8
54/6	24/2	144/12	42/2	54/3	144/12	225/15
25/25	45/3	32/8	54/3	30/6	54/54	10/5
625/25	100/5	32/16	42/7	13/13	169/13	196/14

WORDS

1. BLEEP
2. DUCAL
3. CALLA
4. AERIAL

EASY

144/12	16/4	225/15	63/7	55/5	66/11	18/9
18/5	15/3	324/18	21/3	24/8	54/3	100/10
121/11	324/18	42/2	169/13	20/4	39/3	42/3
256/16	81/9	225/15	60/3	196/14	54/54	42/7
36/6	32/8	361/19	35/7	40/2	25/5	27/9
21/21	28/2	36/2	10/5	441/21	100/10	121/11
676/26	13/13	30/6	15/5	100/4	26/13	100/5

WORDS

1. BUTTER
2. DRUID
3. ARENA
4. CENSOR

EASY

39/3	36/2	76/4	15/3	144/12	100/10	55/5
44/11	42/7	16/4	49/7	529/23	63/9	81/9
169/13	15/5	28/2	20/4	30/2	225/15	72/6
30/5	32/4	144/12	169/13	24/8	324/18	25/5
21/3	34/17	225/15	14/14	54/3	676/26	529/23
576/24	361/19	75/3	60/3	441/21	45/3	60/4
60/5	72/12	35/7	16/8	144/12	42/2	12/3

WORDS

1. BURROW
2. CLOSET
3. DOWEL
4. EDEMA

EASY

16/4	289/17	400/20	10/5	66/6	441/21	324/18
625/25	48/2	72/6	42/6	12/4	15/3	39/3
26/2	12/12	80/10	45/3	576/24	80/4	529/23
40/5	45/5	40/2	441/21	54/3	36/4	12/4
32/4	196/14	144/12	76/4	41/41	12/12	225/15
45/3	1/1	35/7	56/8	15/3	20/10	54/3
84/12	15/3	361/19	14/7	44/44	196/14	18/2

WORDS

1. BARTER
2. ATLAS
3. BLOUSE
4. CARNAGE

EASY

361/19	14/14	324/18	225/15	49/7	121/11	64/8
10/5	100/5	196/14	60/4	54/6	15/3	42/3
144/12	24/12	60/3	676/26	75/3	256/16	45/45
100/5	60/5	14/14	529/23	14/14	72/6	21/3
32/8	36/4	45/9	12/4	16/4	48/4	21/7
36/2	324/18	51/51	38/2	121/11	75/3	24/3
18/9	100/10	4/2	6/6	20/4	441/21	625/25

WORDS

1. ESCAPE
2. ANTLER
3. CLANK
4. BAWDY

EASY

676/26	81/9	15/3	144/12	54/3	21/3	24/6
42/6	121/11	100/10	81/9	441/21	60/3	10/5
64/8	72/8	33/11	36/12	36/6	361/19	57/3
6/2	48/12	60/3	40/2	54/6	10/2	76/4
52/2	14/14	324/18	11/11	9/3	44/11	41/41
144/12	25/5	15/5	225/15	16/4	48/3	54/6
56/8	18/9	36/2	45/3	169/13	30/6	121/11

WORDS

1. DISTRICT
2. COMPASS
3. ARTFUL
4. BROCADE

ANSWERS

PAGE 7

400/20=T (3)						
	36/2=R (3)		35/7=E (1)			
	14/14=A (3)		16/4=D (1)			42/2=U (2)
28/2=N (3)		72/8=I (1)		14/1=N (4)	144/12=L (2)	
	76/4=S (3)	28/2=N (1)	50/10=E (4)		27/9=C (2)	
	39/3=M (3)	48/2=X (4)	38/2=S (1)	45/9=E (2)		
484/22=V (4)	36/4=I (4)	54/6=I (3)	60/3=T (3)		36/2=R (2)	

PAGE 8

	441/21=U (3)			55/5=K (1)		
28/2=N (3)			196/14=N (1)	36/2=R (4)		
	33/11=C (3)		25/5=E (4)	63/7=I (1)		
	441/21=U (3)	400/20=T (4)	36/2=R (2)	60/5=L (1)		
	54/6=I (4)	100/5=T (3)	361/19=S (1)	35/7=E (2)		
		44/44=A (4)		46/2=W (2)	225/15=O (2)	40/2=T (2)
	529/23=W (4)					

				46/2=W (4)		57/3=S (1)
			30/2=O (4)	64/8=H (2)	225/15=O (1)	
	625/25=Y (1)		21/7=C (2)	72/6=L (4)	12/4=C (1)	39/3=M (3)
		60/3=T (1)	441/21=U (2)	18/2=I (1)	144/12=L (4)	36/2=R (3)
			25/5=E (1)	45/3=O (2)	225/15=O (3)	14/14=A (4)
	42/2=U (3)	28/2=N (3)	27/3=I (3)	42/7=F (3)	400/20=T (2)	529/23=W (4)

	20/1=T (1)					
		60/4=O (1)		72/8=I (3)	24/2=L (3)	21/1=U (2)
	75/3=Y (3)	84/7=L (1)	400/20=T (3)		28/2=N (2)	225/15=O (3)
	25/5=E (1)	36/2=R (3)	34/34=A (3)		324/18=R (2)	76/4=S (3)
		324/18=R (1)		324/18=R (4)	15/1=O (2)	
529/23=W (4)		11/11=A (1)	30/6=E (4)	45/9=E (1)	144/12=L (2)	
	14/14=A (4)	80/4=T (4)	40/2=T (1)	48/4=L (2)		

		46/2=W (2)	44/44=A (3)			
	54/6=I (3)	20/5=D (3)	25/5=E (2)	144/12=L (3)		
	60/3=T (3)		13/13=A (2)			
		36/3=L (2)	42/2=U (1)	56/7=H (2)	35/7=E (1)	60/3=T (4)
		256/16=P (1)	400/20=T (2)		60/5=L (1)	72/9=H (4)
		76/3=S (1)	45/3=O (4)	15/15=A (1)	56/8=G (4)	
		361/19=S (4)	12/4=C (1)	441/21=U (4)		

		144/12=L (3)	361/19=S (1)			
		15/15=A (3)		48/3=P (1)	40/8=E (4)	
	36/9=D (3)	72/9=H (2)	324/18=R (2)	13/13=A (1)	529/23=W (2)	36/2=R (4)
	400/20=T (2)	196/14=N (3)	28/2=N (1)	45/9=E (2)		11/11=A (4)
		34/34=A (3)		54/6=I (1)	36/6=F (4)	32/4=H (1)
	44/2=V (3)	529/23=W (4)	35/7=E (4)	72/6=L (4)	57/3=S (1)	

PAGE 13

			361/19=S (2)	42/2=U (2)	6/2=C (4)		
			225/15=O (2)	45/5=I (4)		46/2=W (1)	
	66/6=K (3)	10/2=E (1)	42/7=F (4)	54/6=I (2)	48/6=H (1)		
	30/10=C (3)	72/8=I (4)	676/26=Z (1)	36/2=R (2)	25/5=E (1)		
	27/3=I (3)		12/4=C (4)	20/4=E (1)	44/44=A (2)		
		40/5=H (3)		35/7=E (4)	32/2=P (4)	484/22=V (2)	
		40/2=T (3)		361/19=S (4)			

PAGE 14

			14/14=A (1)	30/6=E (2)			
	48/2=X (3)	400/20=T (1)	27/9=C (2)	60/5=L (1)			
	40/2=T (1)	40/8=E (3)	4/4=A (2)	32/2=P (1)			
	35/7=E (1)	80/4=T (3)	361/19=S (1)	36/2=R (2)	45/9=E (4)		
36/2=R (1)	324/18=R (3)		324/18=R (2)			60/3=T (4)	
	20/4=E (3)			25/5=E (2)	60/3=T (2)	72/8=I (4)	
		484/22=V (3)		529/23=W (4)	64/8=H (4)		

PAGE 15

		20/1=T (3)				676/26=Z (4)
	44/44=A (3)				25/5=E (4)	
	10/5=B (3)	45/3=O (3)	25/5=E (1)	24/8=C (1)	15/15=A (4)	
	14/14=A (3)	57/3=S (1)	15/5=C (3)	38/2=S (2)	324/18=R (1)	144/12=L (4)
		361/19=S (3)	54/6=I (2)	15/3=E (1)	75/3=Y (2)	30/2=O (4)
	196/14=N (2)	225/15=O (2)		400/20=T (1)	60/3=T (4)	

PAGE 16

					144/12=L (2)	
	400/20=T (3)		529/23=W (1)	45/9=E (2)	80/4=T (4)	
		12/12=A (3)	42/2=U (2)	36/2=R (1)		54/6=I (4)
	76/4=S (2)	39/3=M (3)	34/2=Q (2)	30/6=E (1)	400/20=T (4)	
	256/16=P (3)	35/7=E (2)	196/14=N (1)		25/5=E (4)	
	20/4=E (3)	64/8=H (1)	24/8=C (1)			48/3=P (4)
		324/18=R (3)				

					25/5=E (4)	
				35/7=E (1)	45/9=E (3)	54/6=I (4)
				27/9=C (1)	16/8=B (4)	72/6=L (3)
		52/2=Z (4)	441/21=U (1)	39/3=M (4)	121/11=K (3)	
		36/9=D (1)	225/15=O (4)	30/10=C (3)	34/34=A (2)	256/16=P (2)
	169/13=M (2)	20/4=E (1)	60/5=L (2)	12/6=B (2)	11/11=A (3)	
		441/21=U (2)	361/19=S (1)			400/20=T (3)

	400/20=T (2)					
	529/23=W (4)	25/25=A (2)	256/16=P (1)			
	225/15=O (4)		441/21=U (2)	45/5=I (1)	324/18=R (3)	
	16/4=D (4)	28/2=N (4)	196/14=N (1)	48/3=P (2)		40/8=E (3)
50/10=E (4)	361/19=S (3)	32/4=H (1)	24/8=C (1)		35/7=E (2)	60/3=T (3)
	36/2=R (4)	20/4=E (3)	26/2=M (3)	45/9=E (3)	361/19=S (3)	

			32/8=D (1)	225/15=O (4)	35/7=E (2)	
		14/14=A (1)	20/5=D (4)	72/6=L (2)	529/23=W (4)	38/2=S (1)
	144/12=L (3)	27/3=I (4)	20/4=E (1)	18/9=B (2)	256/16=P (1)	
	46/2=W (4)	33/33=A (3)	14/14=A (2)	324/18=R (1)		
		72/8=I (2)	14/7=B (3)		400/20=T (3)	
		484/22=V (2)	54/6=I (3)	36/2=R (3)		

	38/2=S (1)					
		289/17=Q (1)		14/7=B (2)		
		42/2=U (1)	54/6=I (2)	55/5=K (3)	36/3=L (2)	
		361/19=S (2)	44/44=A (1)	28/2=N (3)	40/8=E (2)	
		81/9=I (2)	441/21=U (3)	36/2=R (1)		529/23=W (4)
	484/22=V (2)	324/18=R (3)	20/4=E (1)		72/8=I (4)	
		60/3=T (3)		196/14=N (4)	24/8=C (4)	25/5=E (4)

		40/8=E (1)	144/12=L (1)	28/2=N (2)	15/3=E (4)	324/18=R (3)
			324/18=R (2)	16/4=D (1)	48/6=H (4)	25/5=E (3)
		225/15=O (2)		32/8=D (1)	24/6=D (3)	60/3=T (4)
		21/7=C (2)	42/2=U (1)	42/3=N (3)		72/8=I (4)
	76/4=S (2)		81/9=I (3)	169/13=M (1)		36/2=R (4)
		400/20=T (3)				529/23=W (4)

	72/6=L (2)	33/33=A (2)				
	15/5=C (2)			144/12=L (1)		
		81/9=I (2)			48/4=L (1)	
	625/25=Y (4)		80/4=T (2)	441/21=U (1)		
		45/3=O (4)	27/9=C (1)	361/19=S (2)	75/3=Y (2)	25/5=E (3)
60/5=L (4)	100/5=T (3)	32/8=D (4)	76/4=S (1)	63/9=G (3)	84/7=L (3)	169/13=M (2)
	20/4=E (4)	60/4=O (3)	49/7=G (3)			

PAGE 23

		15/3=E (1)			48/3=P (1)	
	60/5=L (1)	20/4=E (4)	400/20=T (4)	33/33=A (1)		56/8=G (2)
		22/11=B (1)	60/3=T (4)	100/4=Y (1)	196/14=N (2)	
		15/15=A (4)	12/12=A (1)			54/6=I (2)
	225/15=O (3)		169/13=M (4)		75/3=Y (2)	
		44/2=V (3)	12/3=D (3)	44/44=A (2)		
	45/3=O (3)	45/5=I (3)	361/19=S (2)			

PAGE 24

		225/15=O (3)				
	26/2=M (4)	16/4=D (4)	42/21=B (3)			
	60/4=O (4)	38/2=S (3)	45/9=E (4)	57/3=S (1)		
	39/3=M (2)	15/3=E (3)	44/44=A (1)	169/13=M (4)		256/16=P (2)
	324/18=R (3)	35/7=E (2)	54/6=I (1)	144/12=L (2)	56/7=H (2)	
	484/22=V (3)	196/14=N (1)	45/3=O (2)			
		35/7=E (3)	40/2=T (1)			

49/7=G (4)		28/2=N (2)	361/19=S (1)			
28/2=N (4)	25/5=E (2)	28/2=N (1)	72/8=I (2)	625/25=Y (1)		
	45/3=O (4)	15/15=A (1)	144/12=L (2)	400/20=T (3)	45/9=E (3)	169/13=M (3)
	32/2=P (1)	324/18=R (4)	42/3=N (2)	80/4=T (3)		
	14/14=A (4)	30/6=E (3)	72/6=L (3)	225/15=O (2)		
	57/3=S (4)					

	256/16=P (4)				144/12=L (3)	
		36/2=R (4)			225/15=O (2)	45/9=E (3)
	15/3=E (4)				484/22=V (2)	36/2=R (3)
	33/33=A (4)		361/19=S (1)	20/4=E (2)		63/9=G (3)
	27/9=C (4)	44/44=A (1)		324/18=R (2)	28/2=N (3)	400/20=T (1)
		64/8=H (4)	12/3=D (1)	16/4=D (2)	76/4=S (1)	60/4=O (3)
			45/3=O (2)	54/6=I (1)		169/13=M (3)

			84/7=L (3)	25/5=E (3)		
		57/3=S (3)	11/11=A (1)		625/25=Y (3)	
		48/4=L (1)	324/18=R (3)	441/21=U (1)	35/7=E (4)	
		14/14=A (3)		76/4=S (1)	33/11=C (4)	20/4=E (2)
	256/16=P (3)			36/4=I (4)	42/2=U (1)	72/6=L (2)
		361/19=S (2)	144/12=L (4)		48/3=P (2)	
	169/13=M (4)	15/15=A (4)	54/6=I (2)	39/3=M (2)		

					576/24=X (4)	
		56/7=H (1)			25/5=E (4)	256/16=P (3)
			361/19=S (1)		44/44=A (3)	36/2=R (4)
			44/44=A (1)		361/19=S (3)	45/3=O (4)
		169/13=M (1)		60/3=T (3)	12/12=A (3)	48/2=X (4)
	38/2=S (1)		28/2=N (2)	11/11=A (2)	39/3=M (2)	
	36/2=R (2)	225/15=O (2)				

PAGE 29

	625/25=Y (2)					
		11/11=A (2)				48/3=P (3)
		26/2=M (2)	39/3=M (1)			35/7=E (3)
	169/13=M (2)		76/4=S (4)	15/15=A (1)	33/33=A (3)	
	36/2=R (2)	20/4=E (2)	324/18=R (1)	57/3=S (4)	27/9=C (3)	
		529/23=W (4)	54/6=I (4)	361/19=S (1)		225/15=O (3)
	361/19=S (4)		32/4=H (1)	77/7=K (3)	15/5=C (3)	

PAGE 30

		441/21=U (2)				76/4=S (1)
			42/3=N (2)		24/8=C (1)	
	400/20=T (3)	22/11=B (2)	15/3=E (3)	12/4=C (3)	15/3=E (1)	
	225/15=O (2)	196/14=N (3)	39/3=M (4)	32/2=P (1)	324/18=R (3)	
	32/8=D (4)	60/5=L (2)	400/20=T (1)	44/44=A (4)	45/9=E (3)	
45/3=O (4)	60/3=T (2)	14/14=A (4)	20/1=T (4)	81/9=I (1)	256/16=P (3)	
	324/18=R (4)		33/11=C (1)			

PAGE 31

	256/16=P (4)	72/8=I (4)	484/22=V (4)			
			36/2=R (2)	225/15=O (4)	100/5=T (4)	
		25/5=E (2)	48/3=P (1)	30/6=E (1)		400/20=T (1)
		324/18=R (1)	56/7=H (2)	361/19=S (3)	196/14=N (1)	
		25/5=E (1)	55/55=A (3)	40/2=T (2)	35/7=E (3)	
		15/3=E (3)	76/4=S (1)		81/9=I (2)	
	80/4=T (3)				529/23=W (2)	

PAGE 32

		400/20=T (1)	40/8=E (2)			
	45/3=O (1)	48/4=L (2)	121/11=K (1)	45/3=O (3)		77/7=K (3)
	54/6=I (2)	28/2=N (1)	324/18=R (3)	42/3=N (1)	21/7=C (3)	
36/2=R (4)	361/19=S (2)	529/23=W (4)	169/13=M (3)	55/55=A (1)		
10/2=E (4)	15/3=E (4)	28/2=N (2)	144/12=L (1)	11/11=A (3)		
32/4=H (4)	11/11=A (4)	20/4=E (2)	64/8=H (3)	32/2=P (1)		
60/3=T (4)	80/4=T (2)			76/4=S (3)		

		256/16=P (2)					
		144/12=L (2)				38/2=S (1)	
	60/3=T (4)			45/9=E (2)	32/4=H (1)		60/5=L (3)
	361/19=S (4)	12/12=A (2)		72/8=I (3)	15/3=E (1)	45/45=A (3)	
25/5=E (4)	40/2=T (2)	48/3=P (3)		324/18=R (1)	15/5=C (3)		
	21/7=C (4)	625/25=Y (3)			81/9=I (1)	42/7=F (1)	
	400/20=T (3)	196/14=N (4)		36/4=I (4)	36/6=F (1)		

		169/13=M (1)			625/25=Y (2)	
	75/3=Y (1)	44/44=A (1)	196/14=N (3)	24/8=C (2)		
		27/3=I (3)	48/8=F (1)	25/5=E (3)	54/6=I (2)	
		16/8=B (3)	28/2=N (1)		144/12=L (2)	
	361/19=S (4)	81/9=I (1)	36/2=R (3)	45/3=O (2)		
		72/9=H (4)	441/21=U (3)		256/16=P (2)	
		400/20=T (3)	225/15=O (4)	324/18=R (4)	15/3=E (4)	

			225/15=O (1)	36/2=R (1)		
		32/4=H (1)			15/3=E (1)	256/16=P (4)
	10/2=E (3)	76/4=S (1)				45/3=O (4)
	676/26=Z (3)	625/25=Y (2)	196/14=N (1)		400/20=T (4)	
	20/4=E (3)	27/3=I (1)	529/23=W (2)		35/7=E (4)	
		48/3=P (3)	225/15=O (2)	32/4=H (2)	361/19=S (2)	42/3=N (4)
	100/5=T (3)	324/18=R (3)	12/12=A (3)			20/1=T (4)

		20/4=E (1)		81/9=I (2)		
	55/11=E (4)	144/12=L (1)	35/5=G (2)		60/3=T (2)	
324/18=R (4)	56/8=G (1)	100/5=T (4)	15/3=E (2)		361/19=S (2)	625/25=Y (3)
		42/6=G (1)	60/3=T (4)	45/9=E (2)	21/3=G (3)	
		42/2=U (1)	441/21=U (4)	324/18=R (2)		225/15=O (3)
	100/10=J (1)		32/4=H (4)	36/2=R (3)	48/3=P (2)	144/12=L (3)
			400/20=T (3)	57/3=S (4)	72/8=I (3)	

		169/13=M (1)		38/2=S (1)		
	225/15=O (1)			72/8=I (1)		
20/1=T (4)		21/7=C (1)	400/20=T (1)			
	27/9=C (4)				100/5=T (3)	
	15/3=E (4)	196/14=N (2)	76/4=S (4)	324/18=R (3)		42/2=U (3)
	54/6=I (2)	48/3=P (4)	121/11=K (2)	45/3=O (4)	225/15=O (3)	80/4=T (3)
		35/5=G (2)	32/4=H (2)	60/3=T (2)	36/2=R (4)	256/16=P (4)

			32/2=P (3)			
	20/1=T (2)		11/11=A (3)			
		441/21=U (2)	256/16=P (3)	14/14=A (1)		361/19=S (4)
	144/12=L (2)	36/2=R (3)	39/3=M (1)		42/6=G (1)	44/4=K (4)
	63/7=I (2)	81/9=I (3)		196/14=N (1)	20/4=E (4)	
		48/3=P (2)	121/11=K (3)	44/44=A (1)	529/23=W (4)	
		43/43=A (3)	324/18=R (4)	15/3=E (4)	60/3=T (1)	25/5=E (1)

PAGE 39

						60/5=L (2)	
		57/3=S (3)				15/3=E (2)	
	45/9=E (4)	9/3=C (1)	76/4=S (3)		169/13=M (2)		
	144/12=L (4)	225/15=O (1)	25/5=E (3)			441/21=U (2)	
		44/4=K (4)	28/2=N (1)		80/4=T (3)	36/2=R (2)	72/9=H (3)
		36/4=I (1)	15/5=C (4)		324/18=R (1)	361/19=S (3)	45/3=O (3)
		36/6=F (1)	35/7=E (1)		27/3=I (4)	256/16=P (4)	

PAGE 40

			72/6=L (1)		44/44=A (2)	56/8=G (2)	
			40/2=T (2)		45/5=I (1)	36/9=D (4)	30/6=E (2)
		324/18=R (1)	60/4=O (2)		484/22=V (1)	196/14=N (4)	
		225/15=O (2)	25/5=E (1)		15/3=E (4)		15/5=C (4)
	42/7=F (2)	32/4=H (3)	26/2=M (4)		42/2=U (3)	225/15=O (4)	
		60/3=T (3)	45/3=O (3)		39/3=M (4)	289/17=Q (3)	

			25/5=E (1)	84/7=L (1)	18/6=C (4)	
			22/11=B (1)	81/9=I (4)		
		18/9=B (1)	169/13=M (4)	35/7=E (2)	60/5=L (2)	
	14/14=A (1)		1/1=A (4)	32/2=P (2)		20/4=E (3)
324/18=R (1)	5/1=E (3)	45/45=A (2)	324/18=R (4)	196/14=N (3)		
			63/9=G (3)	144/12=L (2)	45/9=E (4)	48/4=L (3)
				36/2=R (3)	11/11=A (3)	12/4=C (4)

						15/5=C (3)
		324/18=R (1)		39/39=A (3)		
		30/6=E (1)		40/2=T (3)		
	625/25=Y (2)		12/6=B (1)	12/4=C (3)	144/12=L (3)	256/16=P (2)
	36/2=R (4)	100/5=T (2)	36/4=I (1)	15/15=A (3)	441/21=U (2)	84/7=L (3)
75/3=Y (4)	10/5=B (4)	54/9=F (1)	36/2=R (2)	25/5=E (2)	16/8=B (2)	
225/15=O (4)	20/4=E (4)	169/13=M (4)				

PAGE 43

	21/7=C (3)			25/5=E (1)	40/2=T (1)	45/9=E (4)
		11/11=A (3)			32/4=H (1)	48/2=X (4)
		361/19=S (3)	32/8=D (4)	44/44=A (1)	40/2=T (4)	
	18/6=C (3)	15/3=E (4)	16/4=D (1)	441/21=U (4)	324/18=R (4)	60/3=T (2)
	44/44=A (3)		28/2=N (1)		20/4=E (2)	
20/5=D (3)	16/8=B (2)	14/14=A (2)		12/12=A (1)	196/14=N (2)	
	35/7=E (3)		100/4=Y (2)	225/15=O (2)		

PAGE 44

			361/19=S (1)			19/19=A (4)
		25/5=E (1)		32/2=P (1)		60/5=L (4)
	76/4=S (2)			15/15=A (1)	256/16=P (4)	
		42/2=U (2)	144/12=L (1)		64/8=H (4)	
26/2=M (3)		36/2=R (2)		40/8=E (1)	55/55=A (4)	12/6=B (3)
30/2=O (3)	12/4=C (2)	36/2=R (3)	324/18=R (2)		11/11=A (3)	36/2=R (4)
	225/15=O (3)	72/8=I (2)	48/4=L (3)	144/12=L (3)	625/25=Y (4)	17/17=A (4)

PAGE 45

		42/3=N (3)	225/15=O (3)	12/4=C (1)	63/7=I (3)	
	40/2=T (3)		324/18=R (1)	169/13=M (3)	144/12=L (1)	10/5=B (3)
	32/4=H (3)	60/4=O (4)	54/6=I (1)	39/3=M (2)	35/7=E (1)	
144/12=L (3)	324/18=R (4)	15/5=C (1)	48/3=P (2)	81/9=I (2)		
75/3=Y (3)	28/2=N (1)	25/5=E (4)		36/2=R (2)		
	30/6=E (1)	40/5=H (4)	30/10=C (2)		42/3=N (4)	15/15=A (4)
			54/6=I (4)	100/5=T (4)		

PAGE 46

		35/7=E (2)		15/5=C (1)	80/4=T (4)	
		625/25=Y (2)	42/3=N (1)	20/4=E (3)	20/4=E (1)	324/18=R (4)
	15/3=E (2)	25/5=E (1)	81/9=I (3)	72/6=L (3)	225/15=O (4)	14/14=A (1)
	121/11=K (2)	32/2=P (3)	63/7=I (1)	48/8=F (4)	169/13=M (1)	
		18/6=C (2)	39/3=M (3)	18/9=B (1)	54/9=F (4)	
		441/21=U (2)		45/3=O (3)	15/5=C (3)	30/6=E (4)
		10/5=B (2)				

			45/3=O (3)			56/8=G (2)
			33/33=A (3)		84/7=L (2)	625/25=Y (4)
			33/3=K (3)		225/15=O (2)	36/18=B (4)
		441/21=U (3)	36/2=R (1)		36/2=R (4)	46/2=W (2)
		225/15=O (1)	39/3=M (3)	11/11=A (1)	15/15=A (4)	35/7=E (2)
	42/3=N (1)		72/8=I (1)	40/2=T (1)	324/18=R (2)	20/4=E (4)
					196/14=N (4)	

		14/14=A (1)	144/12=L (2)			
	12/4=C (1)	11/11=A (2)	196/14=N (1)			
		30/6=E (1)	40/2=T (2)	36/2=R (1)		
		361/19=S (2)	25/5=E (4)	42/2=U (1)		
	49/7=G (3)	400/20=T (4)	75/3=Y (2)	324/18=R (4)	54/9=F (1)	
	60/3=T (4)	45/3=O (3)	324/18=R (2)		20/5=D (3)	
	225/15=O (4)	15/5=C (2)	28/2=N (3)	15/15=A (3)		

						81/9=I (3)
	84/7=L (2)				42/6=G (3)	
	30/6=E (4)	625/25=Y (2)		196/14=N (1)	42/3=N (3)	
	28/2=N (2)	3/1=C (4)	45/3=O (1)			54/6=I (3)
	15/5=C (2)	1/1=A (4)		44/2=V (1)	60/3=T (3)	
	324/18=R (4)	32/4=H (2)	60/5=L (1)	35/7=E (1)		20/4=E (3)
	63/9=G (4)					

PAGE 50

				72/6=L (4)	25/5=E (4)		
	40/5=H (1)	15/5=C (1)	35/5=G (4)		33/33=A (2)	36/2=R (2)	
	12/12=A (4)	56/8=G (4)	80/4=T (1)	16/4=D (2)			
49/7=G (4)	36/3=L (2)		225/15=O (1)	81/9=I (2)			
	196/14=N (3)	16/16=A (2)	24/8=C (2)	324/18=R (1)			
	10/10=A (3)			21/7=C (1)	441/21=U (3)	256/16=P (3)	
		40/2=T (3)	54/6=I (3)	36/2=R (3)			

		39/3=M (2)		36/2=R (1)		60/5=L (4)
		441/21=U (2)		35/7=E (1)	36/4=I (4)	
	81/9=I (2)		625/25=Y (1)		16/8=B (4)	
		28/2=N (2)	144/12=L (1)	36/2=R (4)	55/55=A (4)	40/5=H (3)
			44/44=A (2)	42/7=F (1)	42/2=U (3)	
	12/4=C (2)	36/2=R (2)	25/5=E (3)	324/18=R (3)	361/19=S (3)	
			144/12=L (3)	40/2=T (3)		

	75/3=Y (2)		44/44=A (1)		30/6=E (1)	
24/2=L (2)		36/2=R (1)		42/6=G (1)	169/13=M (3)	
	35/7=E (2)	196/14=N (4)	42/2=U (1)			441/21=U (3)
	28/2=N (2)	15/15=A (4)	225/15=O (1)		72/8=I (3)	
	39/3=M (4)	45/3=O (2)		15/5=C (1)	44/11=D (3)	
	72/6=L (2)	42/2=U (4)		225/15=O (3)		
	32/4=H (4)		256/16=P (3)			

			32/8=D (3)		80/4=T (4)	
		36/2=R (3)	21/7=C (2)		324/18=R (3)	25/5=E (4)
		225/15=O (2)	15/15=A (3)	42/6=G (3)	45/9=E (3)	36/2=R (4)
			324/18=R (2)	63/9=G (4)	54/6=I (1)	324/18=R (4)
		576/24=X (1)	48/3=P (2)	28/2=N (1)	43/43=A (4)	
		45/3=O (2)	25/5=E (1)	36/9=D (1)		
		36/2=R (2)	11/11=A (2)	72/6=L (2)		

		12/3=D (2)	81/9=I (2)	36/2=R (2)		80/4=T (4)
		66/11=F (3)	35/7=E (1)	100/5=T (2)	36/2=R (4)	
		144/12=L (1)	42/7=F (3)	45/3=O (4)	441/21=U (2)	32/2=P (2)
		5/5=A (3)	18/9=B (1)		400/20=T (4)	
	42/2=U (3)		26/2=M (1)	196/14=N (4)	324/18=R (1)	
	34/2=Q (3)		225/15=O (4)	15/15=A (1)		
			12/4=C (4)			

			324/18=R (4)	28/2=N (1)	45/5=I (1)	
		225/15=O (4)	16/4=D (1)	42/3=N (4)	324/18=R (1)	
	36/2=R (3)		12/4=C (4)	56/8=G (1)		
	15/3=E (3)	15/15=A (2)	45/3=O (2)	32/2=P (4)	225/15=O (4)	48/3=P (4)
	60/3=T (2)	32/2=P (3)	256/16=P (3)	144/12=L (2)	36/6=F (2)	
			81/9=I (3)			
		196/14=N (3)				

PAGE 56

42/3=N (1)					169/13=M (3)	
	25/5=E (1)	361/19=S (3)		63/7=I (3)		
	48/2=X (1)		45/5=I (3)	28/2=N (3)	225/15=O (4)	42/7=F (4)
		441/21=U (1)		441/21=U (4)	60/5=L (2)	
		76/4=S (1)	42/6=G (4)		11/11=A (2)	
	144/12=L (2)	54/6=I (2)	72/9=H (4)	35/7=E (2)		
			196/14=N (2)	40/2=T (4)		

	60/3=T (3)	36/4=I (3)	72/8=I (2)		28/4=G (2)	
		484/22=V (2)	324/18=R (3)	196/14=N (2)	30/5=F (1)	
	45/3=O (2)		25/5=E (3)	225/15=O (1)		
	84/7=L (2)	64/8=H (3)		324/18=R (1)		
		42/3=N (3)	44/2=V (4)		56/8=G (1)	196/14=N (4)
		15/15=A (4)	81/9=B (3)	20/4=E (4)	20/4=E (1)	54/6=I (4)
	100/10=J (4)				144/12=L (4)	

	45/9=E (2)	144/12=L (2)				57/3=S (3)
	8/2=D (2)		25/5=E (1)	324/18=R (1)	361/19=S (3)	
	12/3=D (2)	42/3=N (1)		14/14=A (3)	66/11=F (1)	
		36/4=I (2)	12/4=C (1)	36/2=R (3)		
		72/9=H (1)	36/2=R (2)	361/19=S (4)	41/41=A (3)	72/9=H (3)
			76/4=S (4)	84/12=G (2)	11/11=A (4)	
	169/13=M (4)	81/9=I (4)				60/5=L (4)

	20/4=E (1)		40/2=T (1)	256/16=P (4)		
36/2=R (1)		27/3=I (1)	41/41=A (4)	28/2=N (1)	64/8=H (4)	
	56/8=G (4)	324/18=R (4)		225/15=O (1)		
			324/18=R (1)			
		30/5=F (1)	25/5=E (2)	60/3=T (2)		
	42/3=N (2)	36/2=R (2)		196/14=N (2)	81/9=I (2)	
	50/5=J (3)	35/7=E (3)	529/23=W (3)	45/9=E (3)	144/12=L (3)	

	36/2=R (2)			324/18=R (1)	15/15=A (1)	
		225/15=O (2)		45/9=E (1)		60/5=L (1)
		80/4=T (2)	28/2=N (1)			
		25/5=E (1)	27/9=C (2)	15/15=A (2)		49/7=G (3)
		56/8=G (1)			20/4=E (2)	28/2=N (3)
169/13=M (4)	43/43=A (4)	32/8=D (4)	40/8=E (3)	11/11=A (3)	81/9=I (3)	36/2=R (2)
		72/6=L (3)	13/13=A (4)	39/3=M (4)	196/14=N (3)	

324/18=R (3)					
	35/7=E (3)	36/2=R (2)	361/19=S (1)	25/5=E (1)	
	66/11=F (3)	100/5=T (1)	45/3=O (2)		70/10=G (1)
36/4=I (3)	35/5=G (4)	441/21=U (1)		42/3=N (2)	
32/4=H (4)	28/2=N (3)	42/2=U (4)	324/18=R (1)		225/15=O (2)
	56/56=A (4)	15/3=E (3)		45/9=E (1)	56/7=H (2)
		144/12=L (4)			

		27/9=C (4)	35/7=E (4)	361/19=S (4)	14/7=B (3)	
	20/4=E (4)	289/17=Q (3)		63/7=I (3)	76/4=S (4)	22/11=B (3)
	324/18=R (4)		441/21=U (3)			144/12=L (3)
		25/5=E (2)	40/5=H (1)	60/3=T (1)	45/9=E (3)	
			42/6=G (2)		324/18=R (1)	
	24/3=H (2)	225/15=O (2)		34/34=A (2)	54/6=I (1)	
			39/3=M (2)			28/4=G (1)

PAGE 63

				48/3=P (3)			
		60/5=L (1)		15/15=A (3)			
		11/11=A (1)	27/9=C (3)	72/6=L (3)		45/3=O (2)	
		45/9=E (3)	18/1=R (1)	4/4=A (3)	39/3=M (2)		
			225/15=O (1)		25/5=E (2)	324/18=R (4)	
	36/2=R (4)	169/13=M (1)	42/3=N (4)	56/8=G (2)	441/21=U (4)		
		40/8=E (4)		28/2=N (4)	12/12=A (2)		

PAGE 64

	56/8=G (4)					
18/1=R (4)		36/2=R (1)			256/16=P (2)	
45/3=O (4)			225/15=O (1)		25/5=E (2)	
	46/2=W (4)	60/3=T (1)	44/2=V (2)	144/12=L (2)	20/5=D (1)	
60/5=L (4)		72/8=I (2)	441/21=U (1)	28/2=N (1)		
324/18=R (3)	361/19=S (2)			60/4=O (3)		
	15/3=E (3)	48/6=H (3)	80/4=T (3)		39/3=M (3)	

	100/5=T (4)	28/4=G (2)			42/2=U (1)	
	15/3=E (4)	42/3=N (2)		225/15=O (1)		324/18=R (1)
	81/9=I (2)	76/4=S (4)	169/13=M (1)		196/14=N (1)	
	361/19=S (4)	24/6=D (2)		45/3=O (3)		25/5=E (3)
	72/6=L (2)	441/21=U (4)	28/2=N (2)	361/19=S (3)	26/2=M (3)	36/2=R (3)
	63/9=G (4)	12/12=A (2)			54/6=I (3)	

	64/8=H (4)		18/2=I (4)	324/18=R (4)	12/3=D (4)	121/11=K (1)
		15/15=A (4)	36/2=R (2)		14/14=A (1)	225/15=O (4)
		60/3=T (2)		35/7=E (2)	324/18=R (1)	
		35/7=E (1)	24/3=H (3)	43/43=A (1)	484/22=V (2)	
	27/3=I (3)	57/3=S (3)	66/6=K (1)	45/3=O (1)	15/3=E (2)	
	36/2=R (3)					36/2=R (2)
		99/11=I (3)				

PAGE 67

36/2=R (4)				48/3=P (3)		
	81/9=I (4)	8/2=D (1)		25/5=E (3)		39/3=M (2)
	57/3=S (1)	35/5=G (4)	42/3=N (1)	324/18=R (3)	15/3=E (2)	
	27/3=I (4)	225/15=O (1)	14/14=A (1)	361/19=S (3)	76/4=S (2)	
	169/13=M (1)	16/4=D (4)	60/4=O (3)	16/2=H (1)		9/3=C (2)
		20/4=E (1)		28/2=N (3)	11/11=A (2)	
				144/12=L (2)		

PAGE 68

		12/4=C (2)				
	27/3=I (2)			15/3=E (1)		
		40/2=T (2)	676/26=Z (1)		48/4=L (1)	
		17/17=A (1)	76/4=S (2)		42/2=U (4)	
		24/3=H (1)	441/21=U (2)	28/2=N (4)	35/7=E (3)	57/3=S (4)
	324/18=R (3)	169/13=M (4)	18/2=I (4)	324/18=R (2)	361/19=S (3)	
	48/3=P (3)	225/15=O (3)	39/3=M (3)	54/6=I (3)		

		100/5=T (2)				
		28/2=N (2)	40/8=E (4)	25/5=E (1)		
	20/4=E (2)	60/3=T (4)	24/3=H (1)		16/16=A (1)	
	484/22=V (2)	45/9=E (4)	10/2=E (3)	49/7=G (3)		44/2=V (1)
	144/12=L (4)	196/14=N (2)	20/5=D (3)	20/1=T (3)	15/3=E (1)	
	256/16=P (4)	18/2=I (2)		27/3=I (3)		
	54/3=R (4)	25/5=E (4)		26/2=M (3)		

PAGE 70

		54/3=R (2)		35/7=E (1)		18/2=I (3)
		12/12=A (2)	54/3=R (4)	18/6=C (1)	42/3=N (3)	
	60/3=T (2)	225/15=O (4)	28/2=N (1)		80/4=T (3)	
	6/2=C (2)		42/3=N (4)	30/6=E (1)		4/4=A (3)
		15/3=E (2)	12/12=A (4)		32/4=H (1)	88/8=K (3)
		169/13=M (4)	196/14=N (2)		45/9=E (3)	

PAGE 71

			20/5=D (1)		169/13=M (4)	
			25/5=E (1)	35/7=E (1)	45/9=E (4)	
		256/16=P (1)		26/2=M (4)		225/15=O (3)
	75/3=Y (4)	169/13=M (1)	45/3=O (4)			42/2=U (3)
	40/2=T (2)	324/18=R (4)	18/2=I (1)	42/6=G (3)	54/3=R (2)	60/3=T (3)
	76/4=S (2)		15/3=E (3)	15/3=E (2)	12/12=A (3)	
		72/8=I (2)	361/19=S (2)			

PAGE 72

36/6=F (1)			49/7=G (3)	25/5=E (4)		
	27/3=I (1)	42/3=N (3)	144/12=L (4)	54/3=R (1)	361/19=S (4)	45/9=E (2)
	144/12=L (1)	12/12=A (3)	15/3=E (1)	20/1=T (4)	12/3=D (2)	76/4=S (4)
		80/4=T (1)	100/5=T (3)	57/3=S (4)	81/9=I (2)	
		361/19=S (3)		324/18=R (2)	36/4=I (4)	
	441/21=U (3)		48/3=P (2)			72/6=L (4)
	169/13=M (3)					

		54/3=R (1)	60/5=L (4)	256/16=P (4)	39/3=M (4)	54/6=I (4)
	45/9=E (4)	57/3=S (4)	45/5=I (1)	441/21=U (4)	54/3=R (3)	
			256/16=P (1)	81/9=I (2)		15/3=E (3)
		225/15=O (2)	361/19=S (2)	48/3=P (1)	40/2=T (2)	12/6=B (3)
	32/2=P (2)			144/12=L (1)	45/3=O (3)	
			10/2=E (1)	60/3=T (3)		
		60/4=O (3)	9/3=C (3)			

				625/25=Y (3)	54/3=R (3)		
				484/22=V (1)		60/4=O (3)	
144/12=L (4)	32/2=P (1)	42/3=N (4)	63/7=I (1)	196/14=N (2)	20/4=E (1)	121/11=K (3)	
	25/5=E (4)	54/3=R (1)	28/2=N (4)	13/13=A (2)	80/4=T (1)	12/4=C (3)	
			56/8=G (2)	11/11=A (4)		27/3=I (3)	
	45/3=O (2)	324/18=R (2)		72/6=L (4)	16/2=H (3)		
				48/8=F (4)			

		225/15=O (1)				
	54/3=R (1)		100/5=T (1)	361/19=S (1)		
	75/3=Y (1)	15/3=E (3)	54/3=R (3)	72/8=I (1)		
20/4=E (3)	48/8=F (3)		36/2=R (2)		32/4=H (1)	
18/1=R (3)		324/18=R (2)		18/18=A (2)		35/7=E (2)
	48/3=P (3)	11/11=A (2)	40/2=T (4)		60/3=T (2)	196/14=N (4)
	36/2=R (4)	45/9=E (4)	42/3=N (2)	19/19=A (4)	81/9=I (4)	

	44/4=K (3)			32/4=H (4)		
		42/2=U (3)	625/25=Y (4)		72/6=L (2)	
	16/4=D (3)		361/19=S (4)		441/21=U (2)	
	225/15=O (3)	196/14=N (1)	57/3=S (4)	42/3=N (2)		
		76/4=S (3)	15/1=O (1)	45/3=O (4)	63/9=G (2)	
			28/2=N (4)	100/5=T (1)		45/9=E (2)
				12/4=C (1)	24/3=H (1)	

PAGE 77

		54/3=R (1)				20/4=E (3)	33/11=C (3)
	56/8=G (1)	441/21=U (2)	35/7=E (1)	100/4=Y (4)	81/9=I (3)		
	45/3=O (2)	36/2=R (2)	36/18=B (1)	40/8=E (4)	40/2=T (3)	54/6=I (1)	
		12/6=B (2)	42/3=N (4)	25/5=E (1)	12/4=C (1)	361/19=S (3)	
		22/22=A (2)	28/7=D (4)		42/2=U (3)		
	84/7=L (2)	36/4=I (4)		100/10=J (3)			
			99/9=K (4)				

PAGE 78

		169/13=M (3)				40/8=E (4)	
			45/9=E (3)			48/3=P (2)	42/3=N (4)
		12/3=D (3)				324/18=R (2)	441/21=U (4)
	54/6=I (3)		54/3=R (1)			169/13=M (4)	42/2=U (2)
	441/21=U (3)				20/4=E (1)	26/2=M (4)	42/3=N (2)
39/3=M (3)		75/3=Y (1)			60/5=L (1)	25/5=E (2)	18/2=I (4)
			45/45=A (1)				

PAGE 79

	76/4=S (1)	54/9=F (4)		60/5=L (1)		
	25/5=E (4)	441/21=U (1)	36/3=L (1)	144/12=L (4)	81/9=I (1)	
15/15=A (3)	57/3=S (4)	40/2=T (4)	55/55=A (4)	27/9=C (1)	42/2=U (2)	
	441/21=U (3)		45/45=A (1)	15/3=E (2)		54/3=R (2)
	12/3=D (3)	18/2=I (3)	20/4=E (3)	38/19=B (1)	60/3=T (2)	
	15/5=C (2)	225/15=O (2)	42/3=N (3)	361/19=S (2)	35/7=E (3)	
			28/2=N (2)	33/11=C (3)		

PAGE 80

		40/8=E (2)			84/7=L (4)	625/25=Y (4)
	54/3=R (2)			12/6=B (4)		
	35/7=E (2)		24/6=D (1)		39/3=M (4)	20/4=E (1)
24/3=H (3)	361/19=S (3)	32/4=H (2)		324/18=R (1)	45/9=E (4)	32/2=P (1)
	225/15=O (2)	15/15=A (3)		76/4=S (4)	44/44=A (1)	
	18/6=C (2)		36/2=R (3)	361/19=S (4)		
			30/15=B (3)		41/41=A (4)	

PAGE 81

			32/4=H (2)	225/15=O (1)		
			72/8=I (1)	57/3=S (2)	42/3=N (1)	75/3=Y (4)
	40/5=H (3)	361/19=S (1)		36/4=I (2)	16/16=A (1)	38/2=S (4)
33/11=C (3)		14/14=A (1)	55/5=K (2)	22/11=B (1)		256/16=P (4)
	196/14=N (3)		54/3=R (1)	60/4=O (2)	45/3=O (4)	
	225/15=O (3)			54/3=R (4)	45/3=O (2)	12/6=B (2)
		15/5=C (3)		12/3=D (4)		

PAGE 82

		18/6=C (2)		11/11=A (4)	15/3=E (4)	
	225/15=O (2)		324/18=R (4)			24/6=D (3)
	48/3=P (2)	45/3=O (4)	144/12=L (4)	18/9=B (1)	100/4=Y (3)	
	20/10=B (4)	54/6=I (2)		441/21=U (1)		42/3=N (3)
	35/7=E (2)	45/9=E (4)	54/3=R (1)		12/12=A (3)	
36/2=R (2)		28/2=N (1)		625/25=Y (3)		361/19=S (3)
			25/5=E (1)	324/18=R (1)	60/3=T (3)	

PAGE 83

		12/3=D (1)	121/11=K (3)		15/15=A (3)	12/6=B (3)
	225/15=O (3)	46/2=W (3)	30/6=E (1)	18/6=C (3)	72/6=L (4)	
60/4=O (3)			169/13=M (1)	225/15=O (4)	15/5=C (2)	
	24/6=D (3)	225/15=O (1)		38/2=S (4)	66/66=A (2)	
32/4=H (1)	57/3=S (3)		144/12=L (1)	48/8=F (2)	75/5=O (4)	36/2=R (4)
	361/19=S (1)	54/6=I (1)	42/3=N (2)		40/2=T (2)	25/5=E (4)
				12/12=A (2)		11/11=A (4)

PAGE 84

32/32=A (1)		35/7=E (4)	20/4=E (3)	39/3=M (1)		24/8=C (2)
	42/3=N (1)	60/5=L (3)	44/2=V (4)	55/55=A (1)	225/15=O (2)	44/4=K (2)
	12/12=A (1)	12/4=C (3)	324/18=R (1)	24/2=L (4)	60/5=L (2)	
	81/9=I (3)	49/7=G (1)	225/15=O (4)	72/6=L (2)		
	60/3=T (3)	484/22=V (4)			441/21=U (2)	24/12=B (2)
	15/3=E (4)	42/2=U (3)				
	20/5=D (4)		27/9=C (3)			

PAGE 85

		30/30=A (1)	36/6=F (4)			
	15/5=C (4)	42/3=N (4)	12/4=C (1)	20/4=E (4)	16/4=D (2)	
		45/3=O (4)	45/45=A (1)	40/8=E (2)	54/3=R (4)	
		36/2=R (2)	25/5=E (2)	28/2=N (1)		
	18/9=B (2)				80/4=T (1)	100/5=T (3)
			57/3=S (1)	34/17=B (3)	32/4=H (1)	25/5=E (3)
	32/8=D (3)	225/15=O (3)	42/2=U (3)	441/21=U (1)	144/12=L (3)	

PAGE 86

		225/15=O (3)	36/2=R (3)	28/2=N (1)		54/3=R (4)
	42/3=N (3)		42/2=U (1)	484/22=V (3)	20/5=D (1)	45/9=E (4)
	75/3=Y (2)		27/9=C (1)	20/4=E (3)	15/5=C (4)	12/4=C (3)
	16/16=A (2)	15/3=E (1)			40/5=H (3)	196/14=N (4)
		324/18=R (2)	12/2=F (1)			441/21=U (4)
			48/8=F (2)	35/7=E (2)	20/5=D (2)	225/15=O (4)
						22/11=B (4)

PAGE 87

				80/4=T (3)	20/4=E (4)	
	196/14=N (1)	54/6=I (1)	15/15=A (3)	54/3=R (4)		24/8=C (2)
	40/8=E (1)	39/3=M (3)	72/6=L (1)		42/2=U (4)	16/16=A (2)
		60/4=O (3)	625/25=Y (1)	12/4=C (4)	144/12=L (2)	
	60/3=T (3)		72/8=I (4)	16/8=B (1)	75/3=Y (2)	
	42/2=U (3)		48/3=P (4)			48/2=X (2)
		45/45=A (3)		35/7=E (4)		

PAGE 88

			225/15=O (2)	529/23=W (1)	225/15=O (1)		
	324/18=R (2)	52/2=Z (1)	24/12=B (2)			72/6=L (1)	80/4=T (3)
42/3=N (2)		100/4=Y (1)	54/3=R (2)	20/10=B (3)		44/44=A (3)	26/13=B (1)
			169/13=M (3)	36/4=I (2)			
	36/2=R (4)	60/4=O (3)	60/3=T (4)	24/8=C (4)		48/48=A (2)	
		45/3=O (4)	18/6=C (3)			225/15=O (4)	16/4=D (4)

	10/2=E (3)			55/55=A (4)		80/4=T (1)
		36/2=R (3)	324/18=R (4)		361/19=S (1)	12/12=A (1)
		54/3=R (3)	76/4=S (4)	81/9=I (1)		36/6=F (1)
	44/44=A (3)		15/3=E (4)	24/6=D (1)	48/8=F (1)	42/3=N (2)
	28/2=N (3)	14/1=N (4)				30/6=E (2)
32/8=D (3)		15/5=C (2)	56/56=A (4)		484/22=V (2)	
		60/5=L (4)	144/12=L (2)	60/4=O (2)		

	324/18=R (3)	36/9=D (3)			12/4=C (2)	
45/9=E (3)		18/6=C (3)	35/7=E (3)	441/21=U (2)		
40/8=E (3)	15/3=E (1)		54/3=R (2)			196/14=N (4)
		9/3=C (1)	361/19=S (2)		25/5=E (1)	60/4=O (4)
		42/3=N (1)	54/6=I (2)	484/22=V (1)		52/2=Z (4)
		44/2=V (2)	72/8=I (1)		54/54=A (4)	
		20/4=E (2)			144/12=L (4)	30/15=B (4)

		36/2=R (2)	361/19=S (1)	55/55=A (1)			
	324/18=R (2)	20/4=E (1)	625/25=Y (2)	60/3=T (3)	35/7=E (1)	15/3=E (4)	
	10/2=E (2)			45/9=E (3)	48/3=P (1)	48/2=X (4)	
	6/3=B (2)		144/12=L (3)	256/16=P (1)	324/18=R (4)	45/9=E (4)	
		54/3=R (2)	44/44=A (3)	80/4=T (4)	15/15=A (1)		
		54/54=A (2)		48/6=H (3)			
	24/12=B (2)				15/5=C (3)		

		45/9=E (3)	12/3=D (1)	45/45=A (1)	35/7=E (4)		
	60/5=L (3)	55/55=A (1)	75/3=Y (2)	80/4=T (4)	169/13=M (1)		
	56/8=G (3)		16/16=A (4)	42/3=N (2)	36/2=R (1)		
		42/6=G (3)	196/14=N (2)	28/2=N (4)		16/16=A (1)	
	225/15=O (3)	56/56=A (2)			45/3=O (4)		
	2/1=B (3)		24/8=C (2)		24/6=D (4)		

	43/43=A (4)			45/9=E (1)		
		324/18=R (4)	361/19=S (1)		84/7=L (1)	
	11/11=A (4)	28/2=N (1)		15/3=E (2)		48/4=L (3)
	24/12=B (4)	42/2=U (1)	100/5=T (2)		36/2=R (2)	30/6=E (3)
	54/6=I (4)	54/54=A (2)	225/15=O (1)	15/5=C (1)	76/4=S (3)	625/25=Y (2)
	15/3=E (2)	56/56=A (4)	196/14=N (4)		25/5=E (3)	
			16/4=D (3)	72/8=I (3)		

			15/5=C (3)			34/17=B (1)
	12/3=D (2)			36/3=L (3)	35/7=E (1)	54/3=R (1)
		54/6=I (2)	46/2=W (4)	43/43=A (3)	42/6=G (1)	12/12=A (1)
		361/19=S (2)	225/15=O (4)	144/12=L (1)	38/2=S (3)	
	12/6=B (2)			60/3=T (4)	57/57=A (1)	57/3=S (3)
		441/21=U (2)	38/2=S (4)	361/19=S (2)	12/4=C (3)	72/8=I (3)
	6/3=B (4)	25/5=E (4)	54/3=R (2)		30/6=E (2)	

	9/3=C (2)	60/3=T (4)	15/3=E (4)	40/8=E (4)	169/13=M (4)	
	57/3=S (4)	72/9=H (2)		225/15=O (1)	30/6=E (3)	
45/9=E (4)		225/15=O (2)	32/4=H (1)	484/22=V (3)	60/5=L (1)	
	324/18=R (2)	25/5=E (1)	43/43=A (3)	32/8=D (1)		
	43/43=A (2)		12/6=B (1)	324/18=R (3)	20/4=E (1)	
		144/12=L (2)	256/16=P (3)		196/14=N (1)	
	12/3=D (3)	35/7=E (3)				

		66/6=K (3)	54/3=R (3)	54/54=A (3)	18/6=C (2)	
		42/3=N (1)		32/4=H (2)	24/12=B (3)	
	225/15=O (1)	25/5=E (2)		81/9=I (2)	35/7=E (3)	20/5=D (3)
	72/6=L (2)	121/11=K (1)	76/4=S (2)		16/8=B (1)	
			18/6=C (1)	25/5=E (1)		
400/20=T (4)		28/2=N (4)	441/21=U (4)		12/3=D (4)	21/21=A (4)
	15/5=C (4)			100/10=J (4)		

PAGE 97

		60/4=O (2)	60/3=T (1)	55/11=E (4)	49/7=G (4)	
12/3=D (2)	81/9=I (1)	45/3=O (2)	54/6=I (1)	80/4=T (3)	36/9=D (4)	
		225/15=O (1)	529/23=W (2)	36/9=D (1)	225/15=O (4)	42/3=N (3)
42/3=N (1)			100/5=T (2)	144/12=L (4)	24/6=D (1)	35/7=E (3)
		196/14=N (2)	361/19=S (4)		99/11=I (3)	14/14=A (1)
		54/6=I (4)	10/2=E (2)		144/12=L (3)	
	16/4=D (4)		12/6=B (2)			24/8=C (3)

PAGE 98

	57/3=S (2)		30/6=E (1)		45/9=E (4)	
81/9=I (2)		25/5=E (2)		12/4=C (1)	20/4=E (3)	169/13=M (4)
361/19=S (2)	24/6=D (2)		54/3=R (1)		225/15=O (4)	66/11=F (3)
	40/2=T (2)		54/54=A (1)	361/19=S (4)	21/21=A (3)	
		42/7=F (1)		35/7=E (4)	324/18=R (3)	
			529/23=W (4)	43/43=A (3)		
		44/44=A (4)			15/5=C (3)	

	15/5=C (4)		16/4=D (3)		25/5=E (4)	54/54=A (1)
		44/44=A (4)	14/14=A (3)	81/9=I (4)	60/3=T (1)	361/19=S (4)
	25/5=E (2)	32/2=P (3)	54/3=R (4)		12/12=A (1)	
		576/24=X (2)	256/16=P (3)	44/2=V (1)		
		48/3=P (2)	144/12=L (3)	72/8=I (1)		
	225/15=O (2)		361/19=S (1)	45/9=E (3)		
		76/4=S (2)	35/7=E (2)	169/13=M (1)		

PAGE 100

		48/8=F (3)			24/6=D (4)
			55/55=A (3)	15/5=C (2)	441/21=U (4)
	16/8=B (1)		55/5=K (3)	40/5=H (2)	42/7=F (4)
		54/54=A (1)	18/2=I (3)	14/14=A (2)	54/9=F (4)
		324/18=R (3)	57/3=S (1)	15/3=E (4)	361/19=S (2)
60/5=L (1)			32/4=H (1)	54/3=R (4)	80/4=T (2)
	441/21=U (1)	36/6=F (1)		20/4=E (2)	

PAGE 101

	196/14=N (4)	27/3=I (4)	12/6=B (4)			
49/7=G (4)	13/13=A (1)	80/4=T (4)	64/8=H (4)	18/2=I (4)	32/8=D (2)	
		15/5=C (1)	54/3=R (4)	60/3=T (3)	72/8=I (2)	
		225/15=O (1)	45/5=I (3)	42/3=N (2)		
		256/16=P (3)	196/14=N (1)		35/5=G (2)	
	21/7=C (3)	121/11=K (3)	81/9=I (1)		30/6=E (1)	625/25=Y (2)
	9/3=C (3)	45/3=O (3)		60/3=T (1)		

PAGE 102

			36/2=R (3)			
		35/7=E (3)			24/6=D (1)	
44/44=A (4)	28/2=N (1)	144/12=L (3)	39/3=M (2)		45/45=A (1)	
28/2=N (4)	81/9=I (3)	225/15=O (1)	441/21=U (2)	15/5=C (1)		
42/3=N (4)	45/3=O (3)		54/3=R (1)	21/7=C (2)		
	25/5=E (4)	324/18=R (3)			25/5=E (2)	12/4=C (2)
	12/6=B (3)	60/3=T (4)	196/14=N (4)	14/14=A (4)		

PAGE 103

				15/15=A (4)			
		20/4=E (1)		24/12=B (4)			18/6=C (3)
	48/4=L (2)	12/3=D (1)	30/15=B (4)		144/12=L (3)		
	15/3=E (2)		60/4=O (1)	225/15=O (4)	81/9=I (3)		
		484/22=V (2)	63/7=I (1)	40/2=T (4)			26/2=M (3)
		45/9=E (2)		16/4=D (1)	44/44=A (3)		
	16/8=B (2)						48/2=X (3)

PAGE 104

			18/6=C (4)	60/5=L (1)			
	625/25=Y (2)			40/5=H (4)	51/51=A (1)		
		44/4=K (2)	44/44=A (4)		56/8=G (1)		
		361/19=S (2)	54/3=R (4)		25/5=E (1)		
	42/2=U (2)		16/4=D (4)	144/12=L (1)	76/4=S (3)		
		32/4=H (2)			196/14=N (3)		35/7=E (3)
				72/8=I (3)	40/2=T (3)		

					21/7=C (3)	10/10=A (4)
	30/6=E (1)			45/3=O (3)		9/3=C (4)
		39/3=M (1)		28/2=N (3)	32/4=H (4)	20/5=D (2)
		20/4=E (1)	44/2=V (3)		225/15=O (2)	225/15=O (4)
			42/3=N (1)	54/6=I (3)	54/3=R (2)	60/4=O (4)
		36/9=D (1)	15/5=C (3)	169/13=M (2)		324/18=R (2)
		20/1=T (3)			35/7=E (2)	

					27/9=C (3)	
		16/8=B (2)		60/4=O (3)		
			54/3=R (2)	196/14=N (3)	75/3=Y (4)	34/34=A (1)
		34/34=A (2)	361/19=S (3)		72/6=L (1)	36/2=R (4)
	361/19=S (2)	144/12=L (3)	441/21=U (3)	45/3=O (1)		50/50=A (4)
		76/4=S (2)	36/6=F (1)	225/15=O (1)	81/9=I (4)	16/4=D (4)

		18/6=C (2)			20/5=D (3)	
		45/5=I (2)				43/43=A (3)
	196/14=N (2)		625/25=Y (4)	80/4=T (1)	14/14=A (1)	60/5=L (3)
		32/8=D (2)	54/3=R (1)	225/15=O (4)		144/12=L (3)
	25/5=E (2)		225/15=O (1)	484/22=V (4)	15/15=A (3)	
54/3=R (2)		17/17=A (1)		196/14=N (4)		10/5=B (3)
			20/4=E (4)			

	35/7=E (4)					
		39/3=M (4)	25/5=E (1)		21/7=C (2)	
	45/3=O (4)		56/8=G (1)	81/9=I (2)		
		100/5=T (4)	169/13=M (2)	48/4=L (1)		
	15/5=C (2)	45/3=O (2)	15/3=E (4)	54/6=I (1)		
		30/6=E (3)	16/8=B (1)		225/15=O (3)	16/4=D (3)
	60/3=T (3)		121/11=K (3)	18/6=C (3)		

	13/13=A (3)		30/6=E (3)	4/2=B (3)	256/16=P (4)	
		169/13=M (3)		225/15=O (4)	41/41=A (3)	15/5=C (2)
		30/6=E (1)	40/5=H (4)		43/43=A (2)	
20/10=B (4)	72/8=I (4)	57/3=S (4)	40/2=T (1)		48/3=P (2)	
			32/4=H (1)			35/7=E (2)
		196/14=N (1)				54/3=R (2)
			72/8=I (1)	12/4=C (1)		

	54/3=R (1)					
81/9=I (1)		14/14=A (1)			144/12=L (3)	625/25=Y (2)
	15/5=C (1)	44/2=V (1)		41/41=A (3)		56/8=G (2)
	5/1=E (1)		41/41=A (1)	16/4=D (3)	49/7=G (2)	
			42/2=U (3)		42/2=U (2)	
		15/15=A (3)	60/5=L (4)		12/6=B (2)	
	30/6=E (4)	18/6=C (4)	12/4=C (3)	14/14=A (4)	80/4=T (4)	

PAGE 111

	12/4=C (3)	12/1=L (4)		256/16=P (1)		60/5=L (2)
		41/41=A (3)	14/14=A (4)	35/7=E (1)	14/14=A (2)	
		48/4=L (3)	54/6=I (4)	9/3=C (2)	45/9=E (1)	
	24/2=L (3)		42/2=U (2)	54/3=R (4)	144/12=L (1)	
25/25=A (3)		32/8=D (2)		30/6=E (4)		10/5=B (1)
				13/13=A (4)		

PAGE 112

	16/4=D (2)					
		324/18=R (2)			54/3=R (1)	
	324/18=R (4)	42/2=U (2)		20/4=E (1)		
	81/9=I (2)	225/15=O (4)	60/3=T (1)	196/14=N (3)	54/54=A (3)	
	32/8=D (2)	361/19=S (4)	35/7=E (3)	40/2=T (1)		
	28/2=N (4)	36/2=R (3)		441/21=U (1)		
	13/13=A (3)	30/6=E (4)	15/5=C (4)		26/13=B (1)	

PAGE 113

			15/3=E (4)		
		16/4=D (4)		529/23=W (1)	
15/5=C (2)		20/4=E (4)		225/15=O (1)	72/6=L (3)
	144/12=L (2)	169/13=M (4)		324/18=R (1)	25/5=E (3)
	225/15=O (2)	14/14=A (4)	54/3=R (1)		529/23=W (3)
361/19=S (2)		60/3=T (2)	441/21=U (1)	45/3=O (3)	
	35/7=E (2)	16/8=B (1)			12/3=D (3)

PAGE 114

			10/5=B (3)		324/18=R (1)
	72/6=L (3)			15/3=E (1)	
12/12=A (2)		45/3=O (3)		80/4=T (1)	
	40/2=T (2)	441/21=U (3)	54/3=R (1)		12/4=C (4)
	144/12=L (2)	76/4=S (3)	41/41=A (1)	12/12=A (4)	
1/1=A (2)	35/7=E (4)	56/8=G (4)	15/3=E (3)	20/10=B (1)	54/3=R (4)
	361/19=S (2)		44/44=A (4)	196/14=N (4)	

PAGE 115

	14/14=A (2)				121/11=K (3)	
		196/14=N (2)			15/3=E (1)	42/3=N (3)
	24/12=B (4)	60/3=T (2)			256/16=P (1)	45/45=A (3)
	60/5=L (2)	14/14=A (4)	529/23=W (4)	14/14=A (1)	72/6=L (3)	
		45/9=E (2)	12/4=C (1)	16/4=D (4)		21/7=C (3)
	324/18=R (2)		38/2=S (1)		75/3=Y (4)	
				20/4=E (1)		

PAGE 116

			144/12=L (3)	54/3=R (1)		
			81/9=I (1)	441/21=U (3)	60/3=T (1)	
		33/11=C (1)		36/6=F (3)	361/19=S (1)	57/3=S (2)
		60/3=T (1)	40/2=T (3)	54/6=I (1)		76/4=S (2)
	14/14=A (3)	324/18=R (3)	11/11=A (4)	9/3=C (4)	44/11=D (1)	41/41=A (2)
		15/5=C (2)	225/15=O (4)	16/4=D (4)	48/3=P (2)	
	18/9=B (4)	36/2=R (4)	45/3=O (2)	169/13=M (2)	30/6=E (4)	